Spiritual Journey Fellowship, LLC
and
Healthy Journey, Inc.

Presents

Wielding
God's Sword

Praying with Power and Application

J A N I S   M .   B E T Z

ISBN 979-8-89345-258-7 (paperback)
ISBN 979-8-89345-259-4 (digital)

Christian Faith Publishing
832 Park Avenue
Meadville, PA 16335
www.christianfaithpublishing.com

Unless otherwise indicated, all Scripture quotations are from the New King James Version (NKJV) of the Bible. © 1982 by Thomas Nelson. All rights reserved.

All definitions in this book are from *Merriam-Webster's Collegiate Dictionary*, 11th ed.

The cover photo is the Cepher opened to Psalm 91 with a handmade gladius sword. Designed by Janis M. Betz. Photographed by Vista Professional Studios, State College, Pennsylvania.

The information in this book is not intended to diagnose or treat any health issue or to replace seeing a medical doctor. It is your right to take charge and make decisions concerning your health and spiritual issues and needs. By choosing to use the subject content of this book, you assume responsibility for all changes in your health and spiritual status. If you feel a strong spiritual affliction, seek out a pastor, a priest, or a deliverance team to help mitigate this issue.

Library of Congress copyright registration number TXu2-305-843

Printed in the United States of America

CONTENTS

ACKNOWLEDGMENT

I give many praises and thanksgiving to my Heavenly Father, His Son, Jesus, and my helper, the Holy Spirit, for guiding and directing the writing of this book. The Holy Spirit was very instrumental in imparting truth and understanding.

I wish to express my deepest, most heartfelt thanks and appreciation to the many friends and clients who took the time to read this book in various versions and made valuable suggestions. These suggestions have made this book an excellent and active piece of literature. I want to thank my sister, Joyce Hanscom, for her review, computer technical help, and expertise in formatting this book. Thank you to my wonderful and ever-patient husband, Tom Betz, for his ongoing review and editing of every version.

Most of the writing of this book took place in a cozy small cabin owned by my friends Ed and Dolly Hollinger. Many thanks for the opportunity to get away, pray, and write.

My heart is filled with gratitude and love to the Fierce Love 4 Good, LLC group of godly women who hosted me to present this book's teachings in my first woman's retreat from August 26–28, 2022. God blessed this retreat and the advancement of this book mightily. I want to thank all the ladies for their suggestions and advice.

INTRODUCTION

Many Christians do machine-gun praying, where they speak a generic general prayer and hope it effectively hits the target. This book is an instruction tool for those who want to pray more effectively and with greater power in all situations. The goal is to teach the reader to pray like a spiritual sniper. The Bible says in James 5:16, "The effective, fervent prayer of a righteous man avails much." You will learn to be effective and discern precisely the following:

- What is your target or enemy?
- How is the enemy coming against you?
- What spiritual weapons do you need before you go into prayer battle?
- What scriptures do you need to wield to have the most significant prayer effect?

This book covers two ways to wield God's sword in prayer:

- First is covenant, praying God's promises into a situation (Isaiah 43:2; Psalm 91:1, 4, 11–12, 14–16).
- Second is spiritual warfare, praying God's actions into a situation (Luke 10:19; Psalm 91:3, 13).

In Ephesians 6:17, Paul writes that we are to take the sword of the Spirit, which is the Word of God, and put it on as a part of the armor of God. All Christians have a Bible sword, but few know how to wield it skillfully against the evil forces attacking daily. This book will teach you how to wield your Bible sword with precision. How often have you been in a situation where you had an opportunity to share a scripture or felt a spiritual attack and left your sword at home?

I feature Psalm 91 throughout this book because every verse can be applied to any situation you face. For example, while driving an hour home in an icy snowstorm, I prayed Psalm 91:11 the entire way. You can use your own words. This was my prayer: "LORD God, put angels in charge over my car to keep it on the road as well as all the other cars so we reach our destinations safely." Praise the LORD, I got home safely. Knowing Scripture verses and memorizing key verses are essential to pull your sword and apply it when needed. I want to challenge you to memorize Psalm 91 and pray it daily, personalizing the verses. If you have difficulty memorizing, ask God to put the scripture in your mind and write it on your heart (Jeremiah 31:33).

"LORD God, I ask You to cloak the words of this book and its reader with an armor of light (Romans 13:12). Cause the words and God's light to permeate their mind and heart. Bring about a transformation in the prayer power of the reader. I ask this to be fulfilled by the power of the Holy Spirit and in the name of Your Son, Jesus. Amen."

CHAPTER 1

The Power of Wielding God's Sword Praying with Power and Application

I am referencing the "sword of the Spirit" in Ephesians 6:17, which is the Word of God or the Bible. The sword of the Spirit is just one piece of God's armament we are to put on. The apostle Paul stated that we are to take up the whole armor of God. Ephesians 6:13–17 states, "Therefore take up the whole armor of God, that you may be able to withstand in the evil day, and having done all, to stand. Stand therefore, having girded your waist with truth, having put on the breastplate of righteousness, and having shod your feet with the preparation of the gospel of peace; above all, taking the shield of faith with which you will be able to quench all the fiery darts of the wicked one. And take the helmet of salvation, and the sword of the Spirit, which is the word of God."

The Armor of God

Christians begin taking up the armor when we accept Jesus Christ as our Savior. At this moment, we take up and put on the helmet of salvation. This helmet is to stay on all the time. John 10:28 states, "And I give them eternal life, and they shall never perish; neither shall anyone snatch them out of My hand."

As we grow in our faith, we take up the shield of faith to stop the fiery darts that would try to remove our helmet of salvation. This shield needs to stay up and be kept in place to prevent our faith from eroding by adverse events. It tells us in 1 Timothy 6:12a to "fight the good fight of faith, lay hold on eternal life."

As our faith matures, we take up the breastplate of righteousness and seek to live a right and godly life, doing good for others. Timothy further encourages the new followers of Christ in chapter 6, verse 18, to "do good, that they be rich in good works, ready to give, willing to share." Galatians 6:9 states, "And let us not grow weary while doing good, for in due season we shall reap if we do not lose heart."

As we develop righteousness, we desire to put on the belt of truth and share the truths of God's Word with everyone so they may be saved and grow in their faith. Jesus says in John 16:13, "When He, the Spirit of truth, has come, He will guide you into all truth." As we walk and share the truth of God's Word, we naturally put on or shod our feet with the preparation of the Gospel of Peace. This means we need to stand on a solid foundation with our feet protected, teaching the peace of the Gospel, which is the truth of Jesus Christ. We are encouraged in 1 Corinthians 16:13 to "watch, stand fast in the faith, be brave, be strong." The Bible is the sword of the Spirit, where we learn how to be saved, develop our faith, be righteous, speak the truth, and live in God's peace. We are to wield the scriptures of the Bible with precision and power in prayer. Christians should not take off their armor.

Armor Strengthening Prayer

Many people pray to put on their spiritual armor each day. Instead, I want to encourage you to wield the scriptures in prayer to keep your ever-present armor fortified and strong. That prayer may go something like this:

> LORD God, I thank You for giving me eternal life, and I ask that You keep my helmet of salvation on tightly so no one can snatch me out of Your hand. Thank You for strengthening my faith to be a strong protective shield to fight the good fight to quench all the fiery darts of the wicked every day. Thank You, LORD, for fortifying my breastplate of

righteousness and keeping me from growing weary in doing good. I ask that You fill me with the Spirit of truth, be my belt, and guide me into all truth. Thank You for giving me the courage to share Your truth with others. I ask that You will help me put on the preparation of the Gospel of Peace on my feet as a firm foundation to walk in the Spirit of peace everywhere I go. Lastly, I ask that You would give me the ability to wield Your sword with great precision, power, and application so my fervent prayers will be effective and avail much. I ask this to be fulfilled by the power of the Holy Spirit and in the name of Your Son, Jesus. Amen.

Wielding Scripture

Wielding God's sword means using or handling scripture effectively and exerting authority and power through prayer. Scripture is God's spoken word. It contains a divine power and spiritual energy that can be imprinted or applied through prayer to an event or circumstance. Every word we speak has a vibration that edifies and uplifts or destroys and defiles.

James 3:10 states, "Out of the same mouth proceed blessing and cursing. My brethren, these things ought not to be so." Ephesians 4:29 encourages us to "let no corrupt word proceed out of your mouth, but what is good for necessary edification, that it may impart grace to the hearers." Dr. Masaru Emoto, a Japanese scientist, experimented with the impact of the vibration of written and spoken negative and positive words to water. When Dr. Masaru said a curse or blessing word to the water, he flash froze the water, and different shapes of water crystals formed. Positive or blessing words such as gratitude and love created beautiful, ornate crystal structures. Negative or curse words like *fool* and *hate* made chaotic crystal structures. Because the human body is 70 percent water, our words can heal or destroy. In his book *The Hidden Messages in Water*, Dr. Emoto writes, "The vibration of good words has a positive effect on our world, whereas the vibration from negative words has the power to destroy." This discovery is why prayer is effective, brings healing, and keeps us healthy. Proverbs 18:21 says, "Death and life are in the power of the tongue."

Expect miracles when you wield the scriptural sword and apply the power of God's Word to any situation or person(s). Hebrews 4:12 states, "For the word of God is living and powerful, and sharper than any two-edged sword, piercing even to the division of soul and spirit, and of joints and marrow, and is a discerner of the thoughts and intents of the heart." You have the power and authority given by God to wield this two-edged sword. It will help you discern and make a change in your life, others' lives, and this nation. Jesus said in Luke 10:19, "Behold, I give you the authority to trample on serpents and scorpions, and over all the power of the enemy, and nothing shall by any means hurt you." Jesus has given Christians His authority and divine power. I encourage you to apply and use this authority and power in your prayer life.

Wielding the Power of God's Names

The power of God's names can be wielded in many situations. Tony Evans wrote a book called *The Power of God's Names*. In this book, Tony writes, "God is so awesome that He has a name for whatever you're facing. And His names communicate specific attributes or characteristics of God that can strengthen and empower you in your situation. When you discover the name of God that applies to your situation, you will fully uncover the power, potency, privilege, and productivity that comes with that name" (pp. 15–16). Tony lists eighty plus characteristics associated with God's names in his book. The following is just a short list. I encourage you to use and personalize them in your prayer time.

> YHWH (Jehovah): the LORD, the *I am*—the
>   self-existing one (Exodus 3:14–15).
> Adonai: God, Lord, master.

Elohim: the Creator God, God the
      Father—Son, Jesus—Holy Spirit
      (Genesis 1:1, 26–27).
Jehovah Elohim or Adonai: LORD
      God (Genesis 2:4; 15:2).
Jehovah Jireh: the LORD, our
      Provider (Genesis 22:14).
Jehovah Tsaba: the LORD, our
      Warrior (1 Samuel 17:45).
Jehovah Shalom: the Lord is
      Peace (Judges 6:24).
Jehovah Rohi: the LORD my
      Shepherd (Psalm 23:1).
Jehovah Goelekh: the LORD your
      Redeemer (Isaiah 43:14; 44:24).
Jehovah Moshiekh: the LORD your
      Savior (Isaiah 49:26; 60:15–16).
Jehovah Rapha: the LORD who
      heals (Exodus 15:26).
Jehovah Tsidkenu: the LORD, my
      righteousness (Jeremiah 23:6).
El Elyon: the Most High God
      (Genesis 14:18–20; Psalm
      78:56; Daniel 3:26).
El Shaddai: Lord God Almighty
      (Genesis 17:1; Ezekiel 10:5).
Immanuel: God with us (Matthew 1:21–23).
Yeshua Ha'mashiach: Jesus Christ
      (Messiah) (Cepher).
Ruach Ha'kodesh: Holy Spirit (Cepher).

God's names provide power, strength, and protection. Proverbs 18:10 states, "The name of the LORD is a strong tower; The righteous run to it and are safe."

According to the *Zondervan Bible Dictionary*, the name "the LORD" (all upper case) refers to the Hebrew name for God,

"YHWH" (Yud-Heh-Vav-Heh), which means "I am." The pronunciation guess is Jehovah (*Strong's Concordance*—H3068). The Complete Jewish Bible states that no *J* exists in the Hebrew alphabet, so the *J* is changed to a *Y—Yehovah* or *Yahveh*. The Cepher pronounces just the consonants of "YHWH" as (ee-ah-oo-ah) or *Yahuah*. A more common Hebrew name for God is *Adonai,* meaning "Lord" (upper and lower case). *Lord* means "sovereign, controller, or master" (*Strong's Concordance*—H136, H113). Exodus 18:1 demonstrates the difference between the name and role of *God* (Adonai-Elohim) and *LORD* (YHWH-Yehovah). It states, "And Jethro, the priest of Midian, Moses' father-in-law, heard of all that God had done for Moses and for Israel His people—that the LORD had brought Israel out of Egypt." Both attributes of God and LORD did something different.

Power to Act

To have *power* means "the ability to act or produce an effect." It also means "having control or authority." The Greek word for power is *dynamis*, meaning "force, strength, and might" (*Strong's Concordance*—G1411), which is given to us by the Spirit of God. Paul writes in Romans 15:19, "In mighty signs and wonders, by the power of the Spirit of God." We have power from on high. It says in Luke 24:49, "Behold, I send the Promise (Spirit) of My Father upon you; but tarry in the city of Jerusalem until you are endued with power from on high." Luke 9:1 says, "Then He called His twelve disciples together and gave them power and authority over all demons, and to cure diseases." When you become a Christian, you become a disciple of Christ. Therefore, you can receive and operate in the "dynamis" and authority God gives you. If you feel that you lack power and authority, ask for it. To have *authority* means "power to influence thought or behavior, convincing force."

Applying Scripture

Applying scripture when praying for the needs of yourself, others, or any situation has a more significant impact. The word *apply* means "to put it to practical use." For example, if anyone is going through a very stressful situation or troubling times, apply Isaiah 43:2, which states, "When you pass through the waters, I will be with you; And through the rivers, they shall not overflow you. When you walk through the fire, you shall not be burned, Nor shall the flame scorch you." An example of praying this scripture may sound like this:

> LORD God, I ask You to be with the people of this nation as we pass through the waters of this difficult time. Help us deal with sickness and lawlessness so we will be uplifted to rise above the stress and trust You. I ask that You keep the flames of these wicked people and events from burning and scorching us. I ask that this prayer be fulfilled by the power of the Holy Spirit and in the name of Your Son, Jesus. Amen.

Blessing Prayer

Here is an example of applying a blessing to your life and business. Bruce Wilkinson wrote a book in 2000 called *The Prayer of Jabez: Breaking Through to the Blessed Life*. He writes about how praying this prayer can transform your life and attract a multitude of blessings and success to you. This is Jabez's prayer in 1 Chronicles 4:10: "O, that You would bless me indeed, and enlarge my territory, that Your hand would be with me, and that You would keep me from evil, that I may not cause pain [harm]!" The Jabez prayer is a wonderful prayer to apply to yourself, your ministry, or your business to grow and succeed. This is how I personalize it:

> LORD God, I ask You to bless me and my health ministry. May You increase my territory by the

number of people seeking my health services. I ask that You keep Your hand over me, my ministry, and those seeking my help. Keep me and my ministry from evil. Thank You for giving me discernment and wisdom so I may increase healing and wellness. I ask this to be fulfilled by the power of the Holy Spirit and in the name of Your Son, Jesus. Amen.

Now I want to pray and personalize the Jabez prayer concerning how God will use this book to increase His power in your prayer time:

LORD God, I ask that You bless this book and the reader. I ask You to enlarge every reader's prayer territory and understanding of how to wield Your sword. I ask Your hand be with the reader as they operate in greater power to apply scripture to all circumstances to increase their prayer effectiveness. I ask this to be fulfilled by the power of the Holy Spirit and in the name of Your Son, Jesus. Amen.

The following books list biblical references related to life issues, such as fear, worry, trust, etc., followed by applicable scripture to use in prayer. They are *Where to Find It in the Bible, The Ultimate A to Z Resource* by Ken Anderson, and *The Bible Search Engine* by Pamela L. McQuade. The concordance in your Bible is also an excellent place to find applicable scriptures to use in prayer. Choose a verse that may apply to a situation, person, or event and personalize it in a prayer format. As you read scripture, start a personal reference list to refer to in the future.

CHAPTER 2

The Power of Words
and Bible Versions

Not all swords are worthy nor effective in doing spiritual battle. There is power behind words and different Bible versions when doing battle against the demonic and occultic forces. The meaning of a word sets the tone for what is to happen. The spoken word has a vibration or energy that has power over a circumstance or situation. This chapter compares and contrasts critical spiritual warfare words in seven versions of the Bible. This analysis intends to bring clarity and understanding between the versions when doing spiritual warfare.

Word Power

Isaiah 54:17 gives an example of a power word statement. It states that we are to "condemn every tongue that rises against us in judgment." This power statement is in the following Bible versions: Interlinear Hebrew English, Geneva, King James, New King James, and the New American Standard. The same scripture in the English Standard and New International versions writes, "You shall refute every tongue that rises against you in judgment or accurses you."

In the *Merriam-Webster Dictionary, condemn* means "to pronounce as ill-advised, reprehensible, wrong, or evil typically after definitive judgment and without reservation or mitigation." The word *refute* means "to overthrow by argument, evidence, or proof: prove to be false or erroneous." The differences in meaning and power are clear, and condemning every tongue that rises against me in judgment ends all arguments powerfully. To refute is weak and leads to being bogged down in back-and-forth arguments about evidence and proof.

The same scripture (Isaiah 54:17) states that "no weapon formed against you shall prosper," found in the same versions that used the power word, *condemn*. The English Standard and New International Versions state that "no weapon fashioned or forged against you shall succeed or prevail." These two later versions only indicate a weapon specifically forged or fashioned physically. Contrast this to the other five versions that cover a multitude of potential weapons, including the witchcraft weapon that is constantly being formed against us. Jesus Christ has given us authority over every weapon being formed against us in both the evil and physical realms so they cannot prosper. I encourage Christians to operate in that authority, to bind up every weapon being formed against us and command them not to prosper.

Translation Power

The power of Bible translation leads me to another spiritual-warfare power word/translation contrast about the role of divine spiritual weapons in 2 Corinthians 10:4–5. All seven versions state something different, so I will cover the two strongest and weakest power versions. The following are the two strongest power versions:

1) The Interlinear Bible (Hebrew/Greek to English translation) states, "For the weapons of our warfare are not fleshly, but powerful to God in order to pull down strongholds, pulling down imaginations and every high thing lifting up itself against the knowledge of God and bringing into captivity every thought into the obedience of Christ."

2) The New King James Version (NKJV) states, "For the weapons of our warfare are not carnal but mighty in God for pulling down strongholds, casting down arguments and every high thing that exalts itself against the knowledge of

God, bringing every thought into captivity to the obedience of Christ."

The following are the two weakest power versions for 2 Corinthians 10:4–5:

1) The New International Version (NIV) states, "The weapons we fight with are not the weapons of the world. On the contrary, they have divine power to demolish strongholds. We demolish arguments and every pretension that sets itself up against the knowledge of God, and we take captive every thought to make it obedient to Christ."
2) The English Standard Version (ESV) states, "For the weapons of our warfare are not of the flesh but have divine power to destroy stronghold. We destroy arguments and every lofty opinion raised against the knowledge of God, and take every thought captive to obey Christ."

The Interlinear and NKJV Bibles clearly define the spiritual weapons we need to pull down strongholds and arguments, and every high thing that exalts or lifts itself above God's knowledge comes only from the power of the Most High God. I singled out these two battle scriptures because I use them often in combination with spiritual warfare, which is why the power of words and translation must be strong.

Second Corinthians 10:4–5 Prayer

A prayer using 2 Corinthians 10:4–5 might sound like the following:

LORD God, I ask that You bring in every weapon that is mighty in You to dismantle all the powers, strongholds, and arguments of the enemy, along with all the weapons being formed against me. I take authority over them, so they are crushed under my feet. I ask, LORD, that You dismantle any high thing exalting itself against Your knowledge that's coming against and controlling me in any way. I ask that You use the weapons that are mighty in You to dismantle all the trappings and snares that are interfering with my ability to move forward to function in my purpose, my commission, my timeline, the steps You have ordered for me, and the race You sent out for me to run. I ask, LORD, that You would bring all my thoughts back under Your divine control and into the obedience of Jesus Christ. I ask this to be fulfilled by the power of the Holy Spirit and in the name of Your Son, Jesus. Amen.

I wielded the following five scriptures in this prayer: Isaiah 54:17, 2 Corinthians 10:4–5, Psalm 91:3, Psalm 37:23, and Hebrews 12:1.

NIV Discovery and Reveal

In 1998, I took a client to the Oasis of Hope Hospital in Mexico for alternative cancer treatment. The Sunday school message that week was on the differences between the New International Version (NIV) Bible and the King James Version (KJV) Bible. The teacher was a doctor of science and a former atheist. Someone challenged him to prove the Bible wrong, and as a result, he became a Christian. During his spiritual quest to learn more, he noted stark differences between the NIV and KJV Bibles that disturbed him, so he set out to educate everyone he could.

The following are some of the notes that the scientist handed out. At that time, I had a spiritual aversion to reading the NIV Bible and did not know why. This teaching and these notes helped me to understand why. I hope that they will help you see the difference also. I encourage you to look up the following passages and compare and contrast them for yourself. This is just the tip of the iceberg. When the Mexican scientist compared the KJV to the NIV, the NIV omitted sixty-four thousand words, and thirty-six thousand changes were made concerning what God said regarding the following central doctrines of our faith. During a continued study, I also found that the New American Standard Version (NASV), the English Standard Version (ESV), and the New International Version (NIV) all contained omissions compared to other versions.

> Subject: Bible. NIV and ESV omission: "but by every word of God" (Luke 4:4).
>
> Subject: Jesus is the only way. NIV and ESV omission: "of the word" (1 Peter 2:2) and "on me" (John 6:47). Comments: Believe what? Even satan believes.
>
> Subject: Trinity. NIV, ESV, and NASV omission: "Heaven/Father/Word (Jesus)/Holy Ghost" (1 John 5:7).
>
> Subject: Cross. NIV, ESV, and NASV omission: "Take up your cross" (Mark 10:21).
>
> Subject: Devil. NIV omission: "Lucifer, son of the morning" (Isaiah: 14:12). Comments: NIV and NASV say, "O Morning star, son of the dawn!" Revelation 22:16 refers to Jesus as the "morning star." So who was cast down? NIV, ESV, and NASV omission: "Get thee behind me, Satan" (Luke 4:8).
>
> Subject: Jesus Creator and God. NIV omission: "Created by Jesus" (Ephesians 3:9) and "God was manifest in the flesh" (1 Timothy 3:16). Comments: NIV and NASV only state, "He appeared in a body." Who appeared in a body?
>
> Subject: Blood. NIV and ESV omission: "Through his blood" (Colossians 1:14). NIV and ESV completely removed: "But If ye (you) do not forgive, neither will your Father which is in heaven forgive your

> trespasses" (Mark 11:26). NIV and NASV
> omission: "Do good to them that hate you"
> (Matthew 5:44).
> Subject: Judgment. NIV, ESV, and NASV omis-
> sion: "Verily I say unto you, It shall be more
> tolerable for Sodom and Gomorrah on day
> of judgment than for that city" (Mark 6:11).

The NIV and the ESV Bibles completely remove the following fifteen verses from the Bible: Matthew 17:21, 18:11; Mark 7:16, 9:44 and 46, 11:26, 15:28; Luke 17:36, 23:17; John 5:4; Acts 8:37, 15:34, 24:7, 28:29; and Romans 16:24. The scripture in Revelation 22:19 is very clear that "if anyone takes away from the words of this prophecy/book, God shall take away his part out of the Book of Life." The 1984 version of the NIV Bible lists Virginia Mollenkott as a contributor to the NIV Bible committee. She wrote two books: *Sensual Spirituality* and *Is the Homosexual My Neighbor?* She defends the homosexual lifestyle, feminism, reincarnation, and channeling. Virginia calls God a she and Jesus "elder brother." These statements are entirely contrary to the scriptures. This woman should have never been allowed to contribute anything to the NIV Bible. The 2011 version of the NIV has made many pronouns gender-neutral.

A careful examination of the preface of both the NIV and the NKJV helps to understand how each version came about. The NIV preface states that it is an "idiomatic translation," which means it was written according to the language peculiar to a person or group. The NIV had hundreds of contributors, and it went through multiple revision committees, revising the revision of previous committees. Many stylistic consultants further changed its final revision. The NIV preface states this is not a word-for-word translation of the original language. It is a thought-for-thought translation. The NKJV preface states that it is a "complete equivalence" translation, which means the scholars sought to preserve all the information in the text accurately while presenting it in good literary form. The theologian translators of the NKJV signed a statement to hold true to the definition and usage of the Hebrew, Aramaic, and Greek words in their contexts and to use the manuscripts used by most Bible scholars.

Spiritual Warfare Power

My contention with the NIV, ESV, and other simplified versions (e.g., New Living Translation and *The Message*) of the Bible is the spiritual power of the words has been so diluted and weakened in meaning that they are less effective for spiritual warfare. I refer to these versions as dull, single-edged daggers and the KJV and NKJV as sharp, two-edged swords. The following verses are a few examples of this weakening so you can see the difference for yourself:

> *Luke 10:19 (NKJV)*. Jesus stated, "Behold, I give you the authority to trample on serpents and scorpions, and over all the power of the enemy, and nothing shall by any means hurt you."
>
> Comments: To trample means to destroy; this includes all the enemy's power.
>
> *Luke 10:19 (NIV)*. Jesus states, "I have given you authority to trample on snakes and scorpions and to overcome all the power of the enemy; nothing will harm you."
>
> Comments: Trample is just for the snakes and scorpions but *not* the enemy's power. To overcome means to make helpless or exhaust all the power of the enemy. An exhausted power will get strong again and be back to harm you.
>
> *Psalm 91:9–10 (NKJV)*. "Because you have made the Lord, who is my refuge, even the Most High, your dwelling place, no evil shall befall you, nor shall any plague come near your dwelling."

Comments: The conjunction "because" gives a strong reason and connection to the promise that no evil shall befall you. The word "evil" covers a wide range of suffering, misfortune, wrongdoing, sorrow, distress, and calamity. The term "plague" means a disastrous evil and pestilence (destructive infectious disease).

Psalm 91:9–10 (NIV). "If you make the Most High your dwelling, even the Lord, who is my refuge, then no harm will befall you, no disaster will come near your tent."

Comments: The conjunction "if/then" is a weak connection to the promise that no harm will befall you. The word "harm" is limited to physical or mental damage or injury. The term "disaster" is limited to a sudden or great misfortune.

Psalm 91:14 (NKJV). "Because he has set his love upon Me, therefore I will deliver him; I will set him on high because he has known My name."

Comments: To set on high means to lift safely above the situation that prompted the deliverance. To know God's name is to have a close personal relationship with Him.

Psalm 91:14 (NIV). "Because he loves me, says the Lord, I will rescue him; I will protect him, for he acknowledges my name."

Comments: To *protect* is limited to being shielded from injury or being guarded. To acknowledge God's name is only to recognize and admit you know God. There is no relationship.

Matthew 17:21 (NKJV) and *Mark 9:29 (NKJV)*.
Jesus's statement about casting out a partic-
ular demon: "However, this kind does not
go out except by prayer and fasting."
Comment: Fasting is a requirement to cast out
certain demons.
Matthew 17:21 (NIV) was removed from the
NIV Bible.
Mark 9:29 (NIV). Jesus says, "This kind can come
out only by prayer."
Comments: *Fasting* was eliminated as a require-
ment to cast out demons.

Versions of the Bible matter when you are doing spiritual warfare, and I encourage you to do your own compare-and-contrast
research of various versions of the Bible and the power of the words.
I have found that I get the best spiritual warfare, deliverance, and
prayer healing results when I use the New King James Version or the
King James Version of the Bible.

CHAPTER 3

The Power of Christ Crucified and His Shed Blood

It is unpleasant to think or talk about the suffering and crucifixion of Jesus Christ (*Yeshua Ha'Mashiach*), the Lamb of God, on the cross. Jesus's death by crucifixion and His shed blood have power to heal and release satanic and occult holds, bondages, and afflictions. Without the shedding of blood and the sacrifice of Jesus Christ on the cross, there would be no cleansing of sin, redemption, deliverance from evil, and subsequent healing.

Cleanse-Redeem-Deliver-Heal

Christ's cleansing blood brings redemption of sin. 1 John 1:7 states, "The blood of Jesus Christ His [God's] Son cleanses us from all sin." Hebrews 9:14 states, "How much more shall the blood of Christ, who through the eternal Spirit offered Himself without spot to God, cleanse your conscience from dead works to serve the living God?" Sin often invites negative spirits to affect us, such as the spirit of infirmity (sickness). It is essential to confess your sins and seek God's forgiveness to be set free or redeemed from your sins. Ephesians 1:7 states, "In Him [Jesus] we have redemption through His blood, the forgiveness of sins, according to the riches of His grace." We must forgive those who have wronged us to receive forgiveness and the cleansing of our sins. It is important to ask others to forgive us for any wrong that we did to them. Mark 11:26 states,

"But if you do not forgive, neither will your Father in heaven forgive your trespasses [sins]."

Redemption is the payment for or deliverance from sin. Hebrews 9:12 says, "Not with the blood of goats and calves, but with His own blood He entered the Most Holy Place once for all, having obtained eternal redemption." Redemption means to buy back or pay the price. Christ crucified and His shed blood were the payment and ultimate sacrifice to redeem or deliver us from sin. At the Last Supper, as Jesus took the cup of wine, He says in Matthew 26:28, "For this is My blood of the new covenant, which is shed for many for the remission of sins."

Deliverance brings healing. Revelation 12:11 states, "And they overcame him [Satan, the accuser of the brethren] by the blood of the Lamb and by the word of their testimony, and they did not love their lives to the death." It is with the power of the shed blood and the death of Jesus Christ that satan's power of death, authority, and works (1 John 3:8) were destroyed. Hebrews 2:14–15 states, "That through death He [Jesus] might destroy him who had the power of death, that is, the devil, and release those who through fear of death were all their lifetime subject to bondage." Pray and ask God to deliver you from the bondage of fear and rejoice in your victory in overcoming your fear so you may be healed. Fear attracts negative spirit activity, allowing it permission to afflict you with what you fear, putting you in bondage. Pray in the scripture of Revelation 12:11 to help you overcome your fear. Through the shed blood of Christ crucified, we have the authority and power over the satanic and occult holds, bondages, and afflictions.

Healing occurs when Christ's cleansing blood brings redemption and deliverance of sin. Isaiah 53:5 states, "But He was wounded for our transgressions, He was bruised for our iniquities; The chastisement for our peace was upon Him, And by His stripes we are healed." First Peter 2:24 states, "Who Himself bore our sins in His own body on the tree, that we, having died to sins, might live for righteousness, by whose stripes you were healed." By Jesus Christ's stripes and shed blood, we receive cleansing, redemption, deliverance, and healing.

We can plead and apply the blood of the Lamb (Jesus Christ) to situations where we are afflicted and need deliverance and healing. Pleading the blood of Christ speaks to the heart of God. Hebrews 12:24 states, "To Jesus the Mediator of the new covenant, and to the blood of sprinkling that speaks better things than that of Abel." So when we speak to sprinkle the blood or to plead the blood of Christ, God honors that plea and answers our prayer as long as we are obedient to Him and His Word.

Christ Crucified Power

The power behind the image of Christ crucified on a cross is amazing because it represents Jesus Christ's victory over death, thus crushing satan's power of death, authority, and works over us. The power of this image representing Jesus on the cross is particularly offensive to the demonic and occult realms because of the shed blood of Christ that flowed. When we wear a cross that bears the image of Christ crucified, it represents our testimony of identifying with Christ's death on the cross for the forgiveness of our sins and for salvation. It represents the power of the shed blood of the Lamb (Jesus Christ) as a constant reminder of the authority and power we have over satan, and he knows it. It is not the cross that has power. The cross is what many Christians identify with as a testimony of our faith. The cross, by itself, is a symbol of the Roman method of execution.

I have a personal miracle testimony about the Benedictine crucifix. In 2007, I had a client who was the psychologist for a Benedictine exorcist priest. He saw that I had a Benedictine crucifix hanging in my clinic room, and he said that I should have it blessed by the Benedictine priest. I gathered all my Benedictine crucifixes and gave them to him to be blessed. When I got them back, I hung them all up again. When I looked at the crucifix hanging above my desk, my breast tissue became painful; and when I looked away, the pain went away. This physical manifestation did not happen before the blessing prayer application on the crucifix by the Benedictine priest. I called my friend, Father David, a Franciscan priest, and told him what was happening. He said to stare at the crucifix, and he prayed an exorcism prayer to command the ancestral demon and root of cancer to come out of my breast tissue, and instantly, the pain stopped, and it never occurred again. The combination of prayer from both priests and viewing the image of Christ crucified brought me deliverance first and then healing. I have a strong familial history of breast cancer on my father's side. The Holy Spirit revealed to me that I would have greater discernment for spirit affliction(s) and be more accurate when I request my clients to look at an image of Christ crucified, whether it is blessed or not (see addendum 7). This image and the glory light of Jesus Christ force any spirits present in or around a person to be exposed (John 8:12).

Shed Blood Power

I read the book *The Power of the Blood* by H. A. Maxwell Whyte. The author wrote, "I am convinced that the reason so many Christians are living such miserable lives, with sickness and recurring sin, is that they have not realized we must turn our passive theological faith in the blood into a vital active faith that uses it, sprinkles it, pleads it, and recognizes that it is just as effective today when applied in faith as it was in the days of Moses and Joshua. When the blood covers us, and we know it, and we have placed it by faith upon our hearts, lives, homes, and loved ones, then we have created a condition where Satan cannot get through" (p. 70). He encourages people to draw a bloodline around your situation, and satan cannot cross it.

Maxwell Whyte writes many testimonies in his book of incidences of applying the blood of Jesus Christ over germs, burns, injuries, and all manner of sickness, and healing follows quickly. Throughout his book, he writes that there is life and power in the blood of Jesus Christ. When we plead or speak the sprinkling of the blood, we introduce the life energy and power of the triune Godhead into our life, along with its healing, deliverance, and cleansing power.

He gave a personal testimony of when he woke up with an intense sensation of choking, and he spoke the word "blood" three times, "blood, blood, blood," and the choking stopped. God made this statement in Leviticus 17:11 about life in the blood. This scripture states, "For the life of the flesh is in the blood, and I have given it to you upon the altar to make atonement for your souls; for it is the blood that makes atonement for the soul."

The following quote from Maxwell is fascinating. He states, "I have found through practical experience that when people are unable to plead the blood of Jesus audibly, it is a sign that they need strong prayers of deliverance because they are hindered by binding spirits that will not permit them to say 'the blood of Jesus'" (p. 99). He further states, "You can always count on deliverance when you plead the blood. The Israelites sprinkled blood in Egypt and it brought deliverance. Rahab used a bloodline token and it brought deliverance. The high priest of the Old Testament sprinkled blood and brought forgiveness. Jesus sprinkled His own blood and purchased salvation for all mankind. We the New Testament priests serving under our high priest Jesus may now sprinkle blood for forgiveness, salvation, redemption, healing, protection, and victory" (pp.107–108).

Testimony

As I was writing about the power of Jesus Christ's blood, I felt the Holy Spirit direct me to start sprinkling the blood of Jesus into my liver congestion and edema. I immediately felt a release of pressure in my liver. At that very moment, the Holy Spirit gave me a vision of people my ancestors murdered out of rage and anger. I started to plead the blood of Jesus Christ over these souls and the sin trauma memory scripted in my liver and lymphatic system cells and to deliver me from all corresponding spirit affliction connected to the cellular sin trauma. I asked God to send the cleansing power of His Son's blood into the ancestral sin scripting and remove it from my cells and body by the power of the Holy Spirit and in the name of Jesus Christ. Since 1998, I have needed to do coffee enemas two to four times a week to help relieve the pain and pressure in my liver. I have not needed to do any coffee enemas for liver issues since I pled the blood of Christ into my liver on August 14, 2022.

My healing came in a four-part process: First, as a Christian, my sins have been cleansed. Second, I have been redeemed by the blood of Christ crucified. Third, when I sprinkled the blood of Jesus Christ into my liver, it brought a deep deliverance. Fourth, my liver was healed, and I had no more pain or pressure. Hallelujah!

Protection Prayer

The following is a sample prayer of protection and pleading the blood of Christ over yourself, others, your home, or any situation:

> LORD God, I ask You to cover *me/name* in faith
> by the power of the shed blood of Your Son, Jesus.
> I ask that You set a spiritual hedge of protection,
> armor of light, and a bloodline around *me/name*
> to protect *me/name* from the occult and demonic
> attacks. I ask You, LORD, to fill *me/name* con-
> tinually with Your Holy Spirit and presence. I ask
> this to be fulfilled by the power of the Holy Spirit
> and in the name of Your Son, Jesus. Amen.

You can apply the blood of Christ and the bloodline in any situation. The following is just another example of it being applied to this book:

> LORD God, I ask that You put a bloodline
> between this book and demonic and occult
> realms so those reading this book can be pro-
> tected and learn how to be an effective spiritual
> sniper. I ask that You sprinkle Your Son's blood
> over the words of this book and those reading it
> and bring healing and deliverance. I ask this be
> done by the power of the Holy Spirit and in the
> name of Your Son, Jesus. Amen.

CHAPTER 4

The Power of Prayer

Prayer has the power to change and transform any situation or event. James 5:16 states, "The effective, fervent prayer of a righteous man avails much." Praying means asking earnestly for what we lack and need. For example, James 1:5–6 says, "If any of you lacks wisdom, let him ask of God, who gives to all liberally and without reproach, and it will be given to him. But let him ask in faith, with no doubting, for he who doubts is like a wave of the sea driven and tossed by the wind." This is a perfect example of applying scripture to a situation. You can change the word "wisdom" to "love, peace, forgiveness, power, discernment, etc." If you lack the ability to memorize scripture, insert the request "ability to memorize scripture" after the word "lacks." Whatever you are lacking, insert that word after "lacks" and then, by faith, receive it.

Ask and Receive

My friend Sandy reminded me that it is important to insert the words "I ask" at the beginning of my prayer and end with "in Jesus's name." Jesus says in John 15:16, "You did not choose Me, but I chose you and appointed you that you should go and bear fruit and that your fruit should remain, that whatever you ask the Father in My name He may give you."

When I pray in Jesus's name, I know that thousands of men are named Jesus, so I clarify which Jesus I am referring to by saying, "In the name of Your Son, Jesus." I also acknowledge the power of the Holy Spirit to fulfill what I ask. Paul wrote about this power in

Romans 15:13, stating, "Now may the God of hope fill you with all joy and peace in believing, that you may abound in hope by the power of the Holy Spirit."

There is also great power in asking God to have our requests go forth and not return void, to accomplish what God pleases, and to prosper. Isaiah 55:11 states, "So shall My word be that goes forth from My mouth; It shall not return to Me void, But it shall accomplish what I please, And it shall prosper in the thing for which I sent it."

Faith and Fasting

Prayer requires a measure of faith, and the answer to prayer may require fasting. Matthew 17:18–21 says:

> And Jesus rebuked the demon, and it came out of him; and the child was cured from that very hour. Then the disciples came to Jesus privately and said, "Why could we not cast it out?" So, Jesus said to them, "Because of your unbelief; for assuredly, I say to you, if you have faith as a mustard seed, you will say to this mountain, 'Move from here to there,' and it will move; and nothing will be impossible for you. However, this kind does not go out except by prayer and fasting."

We need to operate in faith when we pray. Sometimes, when we pray, fasting is required. Fasting involves abstaining from food for a set period of time as a form of obedience and devotion to prayer for a specific event or situation.

Trinity plus Blood

I have found that it is vital to incorporate all the names of the Trinity—*Elohim* (God the Father, God the Son, Jesus, and God the Holy Spirit)—in my prayer for deliverance and healing. The Trinity brings greater power into the answer to prayer. First, we need to ask

God the Father, who is the supreme power and creator of all things. Second, the power of answered prayer is in the name of God's Son, Jesus, and His shed blood. Third, the process of fulfilling the answer to prayer comes from the power of the Holy Spirit.

A Catholic priest exorcist instructed me that the satanic and occult realms would do evil and curse against all three names. Often, when you pray in only the name of Jesus, the evil activity and curse may continue in the names of God the Father and the Holy Spirit. This activity may be why an answer to prayer is hindered.

The Holy Spirit has revealed to me that the satanic and occult realms will also do evil and curse against the power of the divine blood of Christ to try to stop its power of deliverance and healing. In his book, *The Power of the Blood*, Maxwell Whyte cites a first-hand case where a demon was heard cursing the Trinity plus the blood. He stated, "When Lester Sumrall ministered deliverance to a demon-possessed girl in the Philippine Islands a number of years ago, the demon in the girl spoke in the purest English, although the girl herself spoke only a local dialect. This demon spirit first cursed the Father, then the Son, then the Holy Spirit, and then the blood of Jesus, in that order" (p. 43).

In the Bible, the Trinity plus the blood is written in 1 John 5:7–8, which states, "For there are three that bear witness in heaven: the Father, the Word, and the Holy Spirit; and these three are one. And there are three that bear witness on earth: the Spirit, the water, and the blood; and these three agree as one." The "Word" refers to Jesus as written in John 1:1–5. The Spirit, water, and blood represent Jesus's baptism in Matthew 3:15–17. Jesus told John the Baptist that His baptism in water would fulfill all righteousness. After Jesus's baptism, the Spirit of God descended like a dove over Him, and God spoke from heaven, acknowledging that Jesus was His blood Son. Therefore, the water bears witness to the fulfillment of righteousness. The Spirit bears witness to Jesus as God's blood Son. The blood bears witness to Jesus's death, divine deity, and power to heal and do miracles.

I am experiencing more prayer power and seeing a greater answer to prayer when I speak out the names of the Trinity plus the blood of Christ. I will often further clarify with greater detail who I am specifically praying to because there are many gods (Psalm 82). I will ask the Most High God—*El Elyon*, the creator of the heavens and the earth. I may pray a scripture four times, stating each name in the Trinity and the power of Christ's blood at the verse's beginning. Praying the Trinity plus the blood removes what the satanic and occult realms are doing against all three names and the blood of Christ. For example, I may take Revelation 11:18 and pray it through once in the name of Father God, then repeat the verse in the name of Jesus, Son of God, then again in the name of the Holy Spirit, and, lastly, in the power of the blood of Christ.

Disciple's Prayer

Prayer is more than asking for things. It also involves praise and thanksgiving. Jesus gave us a format for prayer that we can apply anytime. You may know it as the "Lord's Prayer," but it is actually the "Disciple's Prayer." Jesus's disciples asked Him to teach them to pray. In Matthew 6:9–13, Jesus states, "In this manner, therefore, pray, Our Father who art in Heaven." (Acknowledge God's deity.)

> *Praise.* "Hallowed be Your name." (Praise Him.)
> *Priority.* "Your kingdom come. Your will be done on earth as it is in heaven." (Seek God's will.) Prayer of submission.
> *Provisions.* "Give us this day our daily bread." (Pray for needs.)
> *Pardon.* "And forgive us our debts [sins], as we forgive our debtors [those who do us wrong]." (Confess your sins, seek forgiveness, and forgive others.)
> *Protection.* "And do not lead us into temptation, but deliver us from the evil one." (Take authority over the evil one, Luke 10:19.)
> *Praise.* "For Yours is the kingdom and the power and the glory forever." (Praise God for His goodness, blessings, mercy, and grace.)

Breath Prayers

Prayer can be a continuous, open-ended conversation with God throughout your day, praising Him and talking with Him about whatever you are doing or thinking. The Bible tells us in 1 Thessalonians 5:17 to "pray without ceasing." How is it possible to do this? One way is to use "breath prayers" throughout the day. You choose a brief sentence or a simple phrase or verse that can be repeated in one breath: "Jesus, thank You for keeping me up under Your feathers." "Jesus, I receive Your grace." "Jesus, I love You." "Jesus, help me trust You." You can also use a short scripture phrase: "Thank You for always being with me, Lord Jesus." "My strength comes from You, Lord Jesus."

Pray Out, Pray In

I often use the term "pray out, pray in," which means to pray out the negative speaking and thoughts of what you are worried or anxious about and then pray in the positive speaking and thoughts of what you want to happen. Use the verse in James 1:17 as a guide and pray in, "Every good gift and every perfect gift is from above, and comes down from the Father of lights." Pray in what good gift or perfect gift you want to happen. Avoid using the negative words "no" or "not" in your prayer. For example, when traveling in an ice storm, I did not pray that I would not have an accident. I prayed to God in a thanksgiving format to get me home safely, which is what I wanted to happen. When you use the negatives "no" and "not" with what you fear (i.e., accident), you attract what you do not want to happen. I encourage you to read Dr. Fisher's testimony on prayer in addendum 1.

Instead of brooding about what you are anxious or fearful of happening, make your prayer, thought, and speech focus on what you want to see happen. Pray in a connection to the fulfillment of God's promises in the Bible. Speak out these promises, such as "my Heavenly Father cares about me and what happens, and he will lift me up and give his angels charge over me to help me in all my ways" (Matthew 6:25–39 and Psalm 91:11).

Many things need to be prayed out. A typical event I see that needs to be prayed out is "taking offense," which comes in many scenarios and situations. To be offended is the state of being insulted or morally outraged. No matter why you harbor offense, it opens the door to negative spirit activity and worsens the situation. It may also weaken your body and immune system, leading to sickness. Harboring unforgiveness also opens the door to negative spirit activity. Offense and unforgiveness go hand in hand and must be prayed out. Take authority over these two behaviors or any other negative emotions or sins, bind them up, cover them with the blood of Jesus, and command them to leave and never to return. Ask God to put a spiritual wedge and barrier between you and the person or situation generating the offense and pray out all negative effects on you. View this barrier as a plexiglass between you and the person or situation. As you are with this person or in a bad situation, continually ask God to have the negative be absorbed into the ground. Ask God to bring in the good you want to happen.

By nature, we have a hard time forgiving and giving up offenses. Pray for the gift and the ability to forgive and let go of offenses. I like what Philippians 3:13 says, "Brethren, I do not count myself to have apprehended; but one thing I do, forgetting those things which are behind and reaching forward to those things which are ahead." The start in giving up an offense is to put it behind you and look forward to a better situation. Ask God to remove or ground out the emotion of the person offending. Also, continually pray out your feelings of offense. Pray in what you want to happen.

For example, I have a friend who was often offended by her husband's unkind words. First, I asked God to open up her spiritual alimentary canal and drain out all her offenses, negative emotions, and stressors into the ground element. Second, I prayed that God would bring a spirit of kindness into her husband and that he would speak more kindly to her. In other words, we prayed out the emotion of offense in her and prayed in the spirit of kindness in him. She reported that her husband spoke more kindly the whole week. The alimentary canal is another name for the digestive tract, where food goes in and bowel content comes out. The spiritual alimentary canal is a visualization where positive comes in and negative goes out.

Meditation

The Bible urges us to meditate on God's Word, who He is, what He has done, and what He has said (Psalms 77:12; 119:15, 27). It says in Philippians 4:8, "Finally, brethren, whatever things are true, whatever things are noble, whatever things are just, whatever things are pure, whatever things are lovely, whatever things are of good report, if there is any virtue and if there is anything praiseworthy—meditate on these things."

Meditation is often misunderstood as some difficult, mysterious ritual practiced by isolated monks and mystics. But meditation is focused thinking, which anyone can learn and use anywhere. When you think about a problem repeatedly in your mind, that's called being worried and anxious. When you think about God's Word often in your mind, that's meditation. If you know how to worry, you already know how to meditate! I want to encourage you to switch your attention from problems to solutions given to you in the Bible. The more you meditate on God's Word, the less you will worry and be anxious. Ask God to release what you are worried or anxious about and bring in what you want to see accomplished.

Philippians 4:6–7 is a wonderful scripture to meditate on, "Be anxious for nothing, but in everything by prayer and supplication, with thanksgiving, let your requests be made known to God; and the peace of God, which surpasses all understanding, will guard your hearts and minds through Jesus Christ." Pray in God's peace and His power to guard your heart and mind and meditate continually on the gift of being at peace.

Meditation allows God to speak to us. Quiet your mind and listen! He will also speak to us through scripture. Be open to how scripture answers prayer and impacts your life or current situation.

Answered Prayer

Answered prayer depends on a strong attitude of faith, hope, and belief that what you ask will be answered and applied to your situation or world event. In Mark 11:24, Jesus states, "Therefore I say to you, whatever things you ask when you pray, believe that you receive them, and you will have them." The definition of *faith* is "the firm belief in something for which there is no proof; complete trust. It is something you believe with a strong conviction." Hebrews 11:1 says, "Now faith is the substance of things hoped for, the evidence of things not seen." I have a plaque that says, "Faith sees the invisible, believes the incredible, and receives the impossible." The definition of *belief* is "the state or habit of mind in which trust or confidence is placed in someone or something." The definition of *hope* is "desire accompanied by expectation of or belief in fulfillment or success."

It is vital not to doubt because this prevents answers to prayer and receiving what you desire. James 1:6–8 states, "But let him ask in faith, with no doubting, for he who doubts is like a wave of the sea driven and tossed by the wind. For let not that man [person] suppose that he will receive anything from the Lord. He is a double-minded man [person], unstable in all his ways." The definition of *doubt* is "a lack of confidence; distrust; an inclination not to believe or accept." Sometimes an answer to prayer might be "no," or it may not happen until later. The Bible has many examples where the answer to prayer or a promise did not materialize until much later, such as Sarah not having a child until well past childbearing. Pray for patience and trust while anticipating an answer to prayer, even if the answer may be "no" or "wait."

Answered prayer is dependent on repentance and living a righteous or honorable life. When I graduated from nursing school, I was praying and seeking God for direction for where I should go and what to do next in my life. I felt like God was not hearing me. One day, as I was reading my Bible, I read Isaiah 59:1–2, "Behold, the LORD's hand is not shortened, That it cannot save; Nor His ear heavy, That it cannot hear. But your iniquities have separated you from your God; And your sins have hidden His face from you, So that He will not hear." I wept, repented, and committed to following wholeheartedly after God, worshipping Him, and doing His will. Days later, I got a job, and my friend approached me to be her roommate. Two answered prayers in one week!

The word *iniquity* means "a wicked or sinful act." These scriptures list what iniquity or sin is: Numbers 15:30, Psalm 19:13, Proverbs 6:16–19, Matthew 12:31–32, Mark 7:21–23, 1 Corinthians 6:9–10, Ephesians 5:3–6, James 4:17, and Revelation 21:8. Pray and ask God to search your heart and root out sin and sin patterns. Psalm 139:23–24 encourages you to pray, "Search me, O God, and know my heart; Try me, and know my anxieties; and see if there is any wicked way in me, And lead me in the way everlasting."

Paul encourages the believers in Romans 13:12–14, "Therefore let us cast off the works of darkness, and let us put on the armor of light. Let us walk properly, as in the day, not in revelry and drunkenness, not in lewdness and lust, not in strife and envy. But put on the Lord Jesus Christ, and make no provision for the flesh, to fulfill its lusts." I like the idea of putting on the armor of light and the light of Jesus Christ. John states in 1 John 1:5 that "God is light and in Him is no darkness at all." In his Gospel, John 1:5, he also says, "And the light shines in the darkness, and the darkness did not comprehend it." This light refers to Jesus Christ, as stated in John 8:12, where Jesus spoke to them, saying, "I am the light of the world. He who follows Me shall not walk in darkness, but have the light of life." I encourage you to read John 3:19–21 and Ephesians 5:8–13 concerning light versus darkness.

Resistance to Answered Prayer: Appeal in the Courts of Heaven

I was listening to a presentation by Robert Henderson about praying in the third dimension in the courts of heaven. He stated, "If you are praying and hit resistance or there is no answer, look for a legal right against you. Come into the courts of heaven, petition your case against you, appealing to Christ Jesus your advocate (1 John 2:1), repent of iniquity, and ask God, the righteous judge, to remove the legal right of satan to accuse you and prevent your answer of prayer to be fulfilled." He further states, "Third-dimensional prayer is praying to God as a judge to get answers that we have not gotten yet. It is going into the courts of heaven to make your petition and arguing your case to undo the case satan has against you. The moment satan's case against you becomes undone, the answer to prayer will come."

Robert Henderson uses Luke 18:1-8 as an example of a third-dimension prayer to God as judge. This scripture states, "Then He spoke a parable to them, that men always ought to pray and not lose heart, saying: "There was in a certain city a judge who did not fear God nor regard man. Now there was a widow in that city; and she came to him, saying, 'Get justice for me from my adversary.' And he would not for a while; but afterward he said within himself, 'Though I do not fear God nor regard man, yet because this widow troubles me I will avenge her, lest by her continual coming she weary me.' "Then the Lord said, "Hear what the unjust judge said. And shall God not avenge His own elect who cry out day and night to Him, though He bears long with them? I tell you that He will avenge them speedily. "He further teaches that an adversary is one who brings a lawsuit or an accusation to deny what is rightfully yours. Satan/Devil is an adversary, and he has a legal position to come against you in the spirit realm." It says in 1 Peter 5:8, "Be sober, be vigilant; because your adversary the devil walks about like a roaring lion, seeking whom he may devour." To devour means "to consume or to destroy all trace of," as in what is rightfully yours, an answered prayer. Your adversary, the devil, can only devour when he has found a legal right to do so.

Robert Henderson teaches that there are three legal issues satan uses against us before God to stop answers to prayers, "sin, transgressions, and iniquity. Sin is about the intent of the heart and having a wrong motive. This means that an action done with the wrong intent of the heart allows the enemy to accuse you of wrong motives. Transgressions are about activity against God, such as not following God's laws and Biblical principles. Iniquity is sin that is in the bloodline, creating a curse. Iniquity does the following four things: First, it allows the enemy a legal right to tempt you in a given area. Most strongholds come from an ancestral iniquitous root. Second, iniquity will fashion your identity in a way you think about yourself if you let it. Third, iniquity undealt with will deter you from your destiny. Fourth, iniquity will be used to build cases against you in the courts of heaven." King David pleaded to God in Psalm 51:1-2 to "Blot out my transgressions. Wash me thoroughly from my iniquity, And cleanse me from my sin." It states in Ezekiel 18:30, "Repent, and turn from all your transgressions, so that iniquity will not be your ruin."

Appeal Prayer in the Courts of Heaven

"LORD God, righteous judge, I come to You in the courts of heaven. I ask that You would get justice for me from my adversary. Bring in the light of Christ Jesus and reveal to me all legal rights that my adversary, the devil, has brought against me, blocking the fulfillment of my prayer for _________. I appeal to You and Your Son, Jesus, my advocate, to remove all legal rights that my accuser is using against me by Jesus' shed blood and finished work on the cross. LORD God, I repent, and I ask that You blot out my transgressions of _________, wash me thoroughly from my iniquity of _________, and cleanse me from my sin of_________. I ask that all strongholds and spirits from ancestral iniquitous roots of _________ generating a curse be bound, removed, sealed off, and banished from myself and my past and future generations. I plead the blood of Christ Jesus over all legal rights, false accusations, and curses being used against me by my adversary. I ask that they be removed and blotted out. Thank You for avenging my adversary speedily and fulfilling my prayers. I ask this to be fulfilled by the power of the Holy Spirit and in the name of Your Son, Jesus." Amen.

If you know of any sin, transgression, or iniquity that you need to repent of, name it in the prayer, such as the sin of having wrong motives, impure intent of your heart, unforgiveness, holding on to an offense, and anger. If you know how you are transgressing against God, name it out in the prayer, such as cheating, misleading, and lying. If you know of any iniquity, such as giving into temptation and wrong thinking of who you are in Christ, i.e., "I am a failure," name it and repent. Identify and name ancestral iniquitous roots, such as alcoholism, adultery, addictions, etc. Ancestral iniquitous roots may be identified by noting your own prominent, negative behavior associated with a parent such as fretting, worry, anger, gluttony, etc. Chronic health issues such as cancer, heart disease, and obesity may be tied to iniquitous roots. These need to be removed before your prayer for healing can occur. If you feel that there is a block to your ability to be aware of what you need to repent, pray in the light of Christ Jesus and ask God to reveal to you what you need to repent. Note the first word or vision that comes to you.

Sabotaged Prayer

Writing this book has been spiritually challenging. The demonic and occult spirit realm will often come in to sabotage or thwart your request from being fulfilled. I pray to take authority over and bind up any sabotage preventing an answer to prayer. I will go into praise and gratitude for answered prayer many times throughout the day and sometimes for weeks. I praise the LORD and thank Him for giving me the wisdom and knowledge to produce this instructional tool. I pray that you may be able to wield God's sword through prayer with power and application in your own life.

Another reason we may not get an answer we want in prayer is stated in James 4:3, "You ask and do not receive, because you ask amiss, that you may spend it on your pleasures." The power of answered prayer does not occur if your heart's motive and your mind's selfish desires enter your prayer. You get answers to prayer when you do the following, as stated in 2 Timothy 2:22: "Flee also youthful lusts; but pursue righteousness, faith, love, peace with those who call on the Lord out of a pure heart." Also, answered prayer has conditions. Jesus instructs us in Matthew 6:33 to "seek first the kingdom of God and His righteousness, and all these things shall be added to you." The kingdom of God is heaven. In my view, seeking the kingdom of God means accepting Jesus Christ as your Lord and Savior. *Righteousness* means "acting or being in accordance with what is just, honorable, and free from guilt or wrong: upright." Therefore, to seek God's righteousness means to strive to live an honorable and upright life. When you have met these two conditions, then all these things shall be added to you.

Altered-Purpose Answer

Many times, people have come to me, stating that they have prayed for healing but received no answer, or an accident happened, and God did not intervene. The age-old question is, "Why do bad things happen to good people?" Paul struggled with health issues and asked God three times to remove them. Paul says in 2 Corinthians 12:7–10:

> And lest I should be exalted above measure by the abundance of the revelations, a thorn in the flesh was given to me, a messenger of Satan to buffet me, lest I be exalted above measure. Concerning this thing I pleaded with the Lord three times that it might depart from me. And He said to me, "My grace is sufficient for you, for My strength is made perfect in weakness." Therefore most gladly I will rather boast in my infirmities, that the power of Christ may rest upon me. Therefore I take pleasure in infirmities, in reproaches, in needs, in persecutions, in distresses, for Christ's sake. For when I am weak, then I am strong.

God had a purpose for Paul's affliction.

Sometimes, there is a purpose for things that appear bad but lead to good. An illness or accident might have occurred because you are supposed to minister to someone or learn something God wanted to show you. God's answer to your prayer may have a purpose different than what you expected or take longer to answer. Look at the scriptures and listen to what God wants to show or tell you in all circumstances.

For example, I slipped on wet wood and got my foot caught, which caused my foot to twist and hyperextend. This accident caused extensive soft-tissue damage and resulted in multiple tendons disconnecting from my bones. I am self-employed and needed to go to work, so I put my hiking boots on, got my crutches out of storage, took pain medicine, and went off to work. I work in a chiropractor's office. When George worked on my foot, he first touched a vibrating tuning fork on all the bones in my foot to determine if there were any broken bones, and there were none. I asked what I would feel if there was a fractured bone, and he said I would have extreme pain in the break area. Two days later, I went to urgent care, and the X-ray showed no broken bones and multiple tendons disconnected from the bones. I was very impressed with the tuning fork and relayed my experience to a massage therapist a few days later. He spoke about the existence of tuning fork therapy, so I went online to learn more.

To make a long story short, I ordered tuning forks designed to help heal my foot and used them with success. My injury and subsequent answered prayer for healing had a purpose. I have now incorporated tuning fork therapy in my clinics as a healing method for many health and spiritual issues. I praise the LORD for that injury because I now work with a healing modality that benefits my clients and myself today.

Salvation Prayer

Wielding the power of the sword to teach and convince someone of their need for a Savior is the most important act a Christian can do. A question often asked is, "Why do I need a Savior?"

In John 15:6, Jesus states, "If anyone does not abide in Me, he is cast out as a branch and is withered; and they gather them and throw them into the fire, and they are burned." To abide means to have Jesus Christ dwell or reside within you.

In Revelation 3:20, Jesus says, "Behold, I stand at the door and knock. If anyone hears My voice and opens the door, I will come in to him and dine with him, and he with Me." When people open the door to receive Jesus Christ as their Savior, they receive the gift of eternal life. A person must acknowledge that they are a sinner to obtain this gift. To sin means to commit an offense, especially against God. Romans 6:23 says, "For the wages of sin is death, but the gift of God is eternal life in Christ Jesus our Lord." Romans 3:23 says, "For all have sinned and fall short of the glory of God."

Next, they need to confess their sins. 1 John 1:9 says, "If you confess your sins, He [God] is faithful and just to forgive your sins and to cleanse you from all unrighteousness." Additionally, a person needs to recognize that Jesus died for their sins. Romans 5:8 says, "But God demonstrates His own love toward us, in that while we were still sinners, Christ died for us."

Lastly, the prayer of salvation needs to include Romans 10:9, "If you confess with your mouth the Lord Jesus and believe in your heart that God has raised Him from the dead, you will be saved." When we are saved, we will have a helper in the Holy Spirit to teach us how to live a righteous life. Jesus said in John 14:26, "But the Helper, the Holy Spirit, whom the Father will send in My name, He will teach you all things, and bring to your remembrance all things that I said to you." The following prayer of salvation is just an example of wielding the scriptures:

> LORD God, I ask to receive the free gift of eternal life. I open the door of my heart and life to accept and confess Jesus Christ as my Savior. I confess my sins to You and ask You to forgive me. I believe that Jesus died on the cross to pay the penalty for my sins. I believe that You raised him from the dead. Please fill me with the Holy Spirit helper to teach me all things and help me in all areas of my life. Fill me with Your presence and help me grow in my faith in You. I ask all this in the name of Your Son, Jesus. Amen.

CHAPTER 5

The Power of Psalm 91

The world is changing, and many adverse events are happening and are going to happen. The rate of cancer and infectious diseases is rising, and many people are searching for a way to deal with these stressors and events. Pray Psalm 91 personalized out loud. Declare and claim its promises. Apply Psalm 91 to what is happening in your health, your job, your family, your church, this nation, in government, in this world, etc. My friend Karen testified how praying Psalm 91 out loud got her out of a hazardous situation. You can read her testimony in addendum 1. I also want to encourage people to memorize this Psalm to be ready to wield the various verses like a sword to change history.

> He who dwells in the secret place of the Most High (El Elyon) shall abide under the shadow of the Almighty (El Shaddai). I will say of the LORD (Yahuah), "He is my refuge and my fortress; My God (Elohiym), in Him I will trust." Surely He shall deliver you from the snare of the fowler, and from the perilous pestilence. He shall cover you with His feathers, and under His wings you shall take refuge; His truth shall be your shield and buckler. You shall not be afraid of the terror by night, nor of the arrow that flies by day, Nor of the pestilence that walks in darkness, Nor of the destruction that lays waste at noonday. A thousand may fall at your side, and ten thousand

at your right hand; But it shall not come near you. Only with your eyes shall you look, and see the reward of the wicked. Because you have made the LORD (Yahuah), who is my refuge, Even the Most High (El Elyon), your dwelling place, No evil shall befall you, nor shall any plague come near your dwelling; For He shall give His angels charge over you, to keep you in all your ways. In their hands they shall bear you up, lest you dash your foot against a stone. You shall tread upon the lion and the cobra, The young lion and the serpent you shall trample underfoot. Because he has set his love upon Me, therefore I will deliver him; I will set him on high, because he has known My name. He shall call upon Me, and I will answer him; I will be with him in trouble; I will deliver him and honor him. With long life I will satisfy him, and show him My salvation. (Psalm 91, Hebrew names of God as written in the Cepher)

In the book *Psalm 91: Real-Life Stories of God's Shield of Protection* by Peggy Joyce Ruth and Angelia Ruth Schum, it states, "Psalm 91 is the preventive measure that God has given to His children against every evil known to mankind. No place else in the Word are all the protection promises (including help from angels, as well as promises ensuring our authority) accumulated in one covenant to offer such a total package for living in this world. It is both an offensive and defensive measure for warding off every evil before it has had time to strike. This is not only a cure but also a plan for complete prevention!" (p. 57).

Some of the following information in this instructional tool is from Peggy Ruth and Angelia Schum, along with the discernment I sought in prayer. Peggy and Angelia write real-life stories of God's shield of protection and what this Psalm means for you and those you love. It is essential to know that within Psalm 91 scripture, conditions must be met to receive the promises. You must first do your part, and then God will fulfill His part.

(1) "He who dwells in the secret place of the Most High (El Elyon) shall abide under the shadow of the Almighty (El Shaddai)." The first verse talks about dwelling in the secret place of the Most High, much like entering a safe place. For me, this means praying, reading, and obeying the Bible's teachings daily. Peggy and Angelia state, "The secret place is, in reality, the intimacy and familiarity of the presence of God Himself" (p. 8). It is then that we abide under God's shadow so the demonic, occult realms can't see us.

(2) "I will say of the LORD (Yahuah), 'He is my refuge and my fortress; My God (Elohiym), in Him I will trust.'" The second verse encourages you to speak out loud your acknowledgment of who God is to you and your trust in Him. The more you say this, the more confidence in God's protection you will have during a crisis or times of trouble. *Refuge* means "to have shelter or protection from danger or distress or a place that provides shelter or protection" (*Merriam-Webster's Collegiate Dictionary*). Psalm 18:2 states, "The LORD is my rock and my fortress and my deliverer; My God, my strength, in whom I will trust; My shield and the horn of my salvation, my stronghold." Peggy and Angelia write, "God Himself becomes the defensive site for us against all invading enemies. He is personally our protection" (p. 12). There are four invading spiritual enemies, which are listed in Ephesians 6:12, "For we do not wrestle against flesh and blood, but against [1] principalities, against [2] powers, against the [3] rulers of the darkness of this age, against [4] spiritual hosts of wickedness in the heavenly places."

(3) "Surely He shall deliver you from the snare of the fowler, and from the perilous pestilence." A *fowler* "is a trapper who sets snares/traps to capture an animal or bird." Snares are specifically set on purpose with the intent to destroy,

which is what your Ephesians 6:12 spiritual enemies do to us. Second Timothy 2:26 states, "And that they [a servant of the Lord] may come to their senses and escape the snare of the devil, having been taken captive by him to do his will." Peggy and Angelia write, "The traps that are set for us are not there by accident. It is as if the trap has your name on it. They are custom-made and baited specifically for each one of us" (p. 17). They continue to say, "The enemy knows exactly what will most likely hook us, and he knows exactly which thought to put into our minds to lure us into the trap" (p. 18). Snares come in many forms, such as unforgiveness (2 Corinthians 2:10–11), lack of self-control (1 Corinthians 7:5), anger (Ephesians 4:26–27), sexual immorality, testing Christ, and complaining (1 Corinthians 10:8–10). Psalm 31:4 states, "Pull me out of the net which they have secretly laid for me, for You are my strength."

Pestilence is defined in the *Merriam-Webster's Collegiate Dictionary* as "a contagious or infectious epidemic disease that is virulent and devastating; something that is destructive." *Perilous* is defined as "full of or involving peril—exposure to the risk of being injured, destroyed, or lost." Your spiritual enemies will often use pestilence to bring destruction to your body. To remedy this, you, first, take authority over your sickness and disease (Luke 10:19); second, command or decree it to leave your body in the name of Jesus Christ and by the power of His blood and the Holy Spirit; and third, claim and declare your healing and the promise that God will deliver you from this pestilence.

(4) "He shall cover you with His feathers, and under His wings you shall take refuge; His truth shall be your shield and buckler." Have you ever seen a hen with her chicks when a hawk was flying overhead? The hen will call out, and her chicks run under her outstretched wings. This is what God does when there is trouble. He will call you to get up under His outstretched wing. When you are under His wing,

it is harder for spiritual enemies to get to you. They will lay snares to lure you out, to trap and destroy you. Jesus says in John 10:10, "The thief [i.e., fowler] does not come except to steal, and to kill, and to destroy. I have come that they may have life, and that they may have it more abundantly." Your spiritual enemies want to destroy you, so stay under God's wing and pray for Jesus's abundant life. You remain under God's wing by having a relationship with Him through prayer, reading your Bible, and having your thoughts focused on Him. It says in Isaiah 26:3, "You [God] will keep him in perfect peace, whose mind is stayed on You, because he trusts in You." You also get protection when you seek God's truth, which is God's Living and Written Word, and your shield and buckler. A buckler is another word for a shield. Pray for and visualize God's wing over you and the Word of God coming between you and the enemy like a shield.

(5–6) "You shall not be afraid of the terror by night, nor of the arrow that flies by day, nor of the pestilence that walks in darkness, nor of the destruction that lays waste at noonday." Peggy and Angelia note that "verses 5–6 of Psalm 91 cover an entire twenty-four-hour period, emphasizing day-and-night protection. But what is more important is that these two verses encompass every evil known to man" (p. 35). They continue to state that "fear is the opposite of faith, and fear will keep us from operating in the faith" (p. 36). Faith believes that God will fulfill all His promises in Psalm 91 so you will not need to fear or worry about anything. 1 John 4:18 states, "There is no fear in love; but perfect love casts out fear, because fear involves torment. But he who fears has not been made perfect in love." Jesus Christ and His death on the cross is His perfect love for humanity. I encourage you to pray and ask for Christ's perfect love to replace your fear or worry. Second Timothy 1:7 states, "For God has not given us a spirit of fear, but of power and of love and of a sound mind." Continue to pray and ask God to give you power and a sound mind to deal with fear, anxiety, and worry.

Terror by night brings destruction against righteous and good people through evil and wicked people. Psalms 37:14–15 states, "The wicked have drawn the sword and have bent their bow, to cast down the poor and needy, to slay those who are of upright conduct. Their sword shall enter their own heart, and their bows shall be broken." *Arrows that fly by day* are anything that pierces or wounds spiritually, physically, mentally, emotionally, and financially. Arrows may also be a negatively spoken word. James 3:8–10 states, "But no man can tame the tongue. It is an unruly evil, full of deadly poison. With it we bless our God and Father, and with it we curse men, who have been made in the similitude of God. Out of the same mouth proceed blessing and cursing. My brethren, these things ought not to be so." *Pestilence that walks in darkness* may represent disease and cancer to destroy your health. *Destruction that lays waste at noonday* are events people have no control over, such as floods, fires, earthquakes, tornadoes, volcanoes, war, etc. We can pray concerning these events like Jesus did concerning the storm in Mark 4:39 when He rebuked the winds and waves, and they stopped.

Peggy and Angelia point out, "There is a difference between the destruction of the enemy and persecution for the gospel's sake." Paul writes in 2 Timothy 3:12, "All who desire to live godly in Christ Jesus will suffer persecution." There are times when we will be mistreated because of our stand for the cause of Christ" (p. 58). In John 15:19–20, Jesus states, "If you were of the world, the world would love its own. Yet because you are not of the world, but I chose you out of the world; therefore the world hates you. Remember the word that I said to you, a servant is not greater than his master. If they persecuted Me, they will also persecute you. If they kept My word, they will keep yours also." Jesus knew that Christians were going to be harmed, persecuted, and killed when He said in Mark 16:18, "They [believers] will take up serpents; and if they drink anything deadly, it will by no means hurt them; they will lay hands on the sick, and they will recover." I love these promises! Serpents may represent any poison or inoculation injected into us. There are also a lot of chemical poisons in the food and water supply that may cause cancer and illnesses. I encourage you to claim the promise that it will be rendered harmless.

(7–8) "A thousand may fall at your side, and ten thousand at your right hand; but it shall not come near you. Only with your eyes shall you look, and see the reward of the wicked." As verses 5 and 6 are happening, you need to trust God that it will not come near you, or if it does, trust God that He will see you through the events of verses 5 and 6. Trust means "to place confidence: depend; to commit or place in one's care or keeping" (*Merriam-Webster's Collegiate Dictionary*). Isaiah 43:2 states, "When you pass through the waters, I will be with you; And through the rivers, they shall not overflow you. When you walk through the fire, you shall not be burned, Nor shall the flame scorch you."

The reward will not be for the good of the wicked. What will be happening to the wicked is written all through Scripture. Read Psalm 37 for an example (see addendum 4). I will pray, applying Revelation 11:18 to the wicked and spiritual enemies. Peggy and Angelia write, "The justice of God is that evil will not triumph; that Hitlers do not win, that communistic governments fall, that darkness does not extinguish light" (p. 57). They further write, "The word only denotes a protection of only seeing and not experiencing the evil, and it denotes detachment in that the evil we see does not get inside of us" (p. 57).

I like to visualize that I am on a spiritual "ark," so when God rains down His wrath and destruction on the wicked, I will be protected on the spiritual "ark," watching the reward of the wicked. It says in 2 Timothy 4:18, "And the

Lord will deliver me from every evil work and preserve me for His heavenly kingdom. To Him be glory forever and ever. Amen!"

(9–10) "Because you have made the LORD (Yahuah), who is my refuge, Even the Most High (El Elyon), your dwelling place, No evil shall befall you, nor shall any plague come near your dwelling." This verse is an example of meeting a condition to get a promise. You need to be a dwelling place for the LORD to live. In other words, you need to verbally ask the LORD to come into your being, your life, and all you do to be your refuge and your Most High God, whom you trust and go to for help. In Revelation 3:20, Jesus says, "Behold, I stand at the door and knock. If anyone hears My voice and opens the door, I will come in to him [i.e., dwell] and dine with him, and he with Me [i.e., have a relationship]." Romans 10:9–10 states, "That if you confess with your mouth the Lord Jesus and believe in your heart that God has raised Him from the dead, you will be saved. For with the heart one believes unto righteousness, and with the mouth confession is made unto salvation." When Jesus Christ is Lord of your life, He lives inside of you, then He says that no evil will overtake you nor any plague will come near your dwelling (body). *Plague* means "a disastrous evil or affliction: calamity; an epidemic disease causing a high rate of mortality: pestilence" (*Merriam-Webster's Collegiate Dictionary*). You can take authority over evil and plagues and command them to leave.

(11–12) "For He shall give His angels charge over you, to keep you in all your ways. In their hands they shall bear you up, lest you dash your foot against a stone." These verses are self-explanatory. Angels are ministering spirits (Hebrews 1:13–14), and you can ask God what you need the angels to do every day and in every situation (e.g., driving, working) and thank Him for sending them to you to fulfill these verses, especially against the conditions of verses 5–6. Pray specifically to God to have the angels keep you from terror, arrows, pestilence, and destruction. The best book on angels that I have read is by Billy Graham called *Angels*.

(13) "You shall tread upon the lion and the cobra, the young lion and the serpent you shall trample underfoot." In Luke 10:19, Jesus states, "Behold, I give you the authority to trample on serpents and scorpions, and over all the power of the enemy, and nothing shall by any means hurt you." Jesus says that you, as a Christian, have authority over these spiritual enemies, along with the spiritual enemies of Ephesians 6:12, and everything they are trying to do to you (i.e., incite sickness). They do not have authority over you unless there is sin, which will give the demonic permission to afflict you.

Interestingly, four entities are listed: lion, cobra, young lion, and serpent/dragon, representing different means of attack or problems you may face.

The devil is likened to a lion in 1 Peter 5:8. "Be sober, be vigilant; because your adversary the devil walks about like a roaring lion, seeking whom he may devour [destroy]."

A cobra is sneaky, waiting to strike you when you least suspect an attack. It injects venom into you to poison and destroy you. You may think all is well, and then you get the diagnosis. The cobra poison that incites health problems is in many aspects of your life. It is in pharmaceuticals and your food, such as genetically modified foods (wheat, corn, soy, barley, and alfalfa), chemicals, toxins, etc. Sugar and simple carbohydrates (e.g., white flour, white rice, and potatoes) weaken your immune system and fertilize cancer cells. Many prescription drugs and inoculations contain toxic chemicals entering your body's tissues and systems. Bill Gates has done several presentations where he openly proposed using inoculations to control population growth.

A young lion grows up to be a big lion. A young lion is a minor sin that you entertain, and the more you feed this sin (i.e., keep covering it up), the bigger it grows. When fully grown, it devastates your life. The truth will come out. Your lies and cover-ups will be exposed, and your career or family may be devastated. Holding onto the sin of unforgiveness, bitterness, anger, etc. may stimulate sickness and cancer. Katie Souza, author and speaker on soul wounds, says that these sins become soul wounds, and you need to bring the blood and the glory light of Jesus Christ down into these sin-created soul wounds and release them to receive healing. See addendum 6 for more information.

The serpent refers to a dragon in the King James Version. A serpent or dragon generates fear. When you allow fear to enter your thinking, it consumes you and paralyzes you. You become a captive of fear, and it squeezes the life out of you.

When you encounter the lion, cobra, young lion, and serpent, take authority over them, ask God to bind them up and remove them, put them under your feet, and be free from them in the name of the Father, the Son, Jesus, and the Holy Spirit. When you read the Bible, you learn the schemes and devices of these four entities, so you know how to escape or avoid them. Second Corinthians 2:11 states, "Lest Satan should take advantage of us; for we are not ignorant of his devices."

(14) "Because he has set his love upon Me, therefore I will deliver him; I will set him on high because he has known My name." Here is another condition to a promise. You must first love God, and then He will deliver you. Peggy and Angelia write, "Love is the cohesiveness that binds man to God, and God will be faithful to His beloved. Love always requires presence and nearness" (p. 78). God longs for you to love Him and express your love for Him. As His expression of love back to you, He will deliver you and set you on high because you know His name. In other words, you have such a loving relationship with God and His Son, Jesus, that you know everything about Him through read-

ing His Word. When He sets you on high, He is raising you above the wiles of the adversary, the devil. You are up on the spiritual mountaintop and out of range from an attack. God says He will protect and deliver or save you from everything in verses 5, 6, and 13.

(15–16) "He shall call upon Me, and I will answer him; I will be with him in trouble; I will deliver him and honor him. With long life I will satisfy him, and show him My salvation." Here, again, is a condition to a promise. Throughout the Bible, it states that when you call out to or come to God, He will answer you, be with you in trouble, deliver you, honor you (show favor), satisfy you with long life, and save you from everything in verses 5, 6, and 13. It says in 1 John 5:14–15, "Now this is the confidence that we have in Him, that if we ask anything according to His will, He hears us. And if we know that He hears us, whatever we ask, we know that we have the petitions that we have asked of Him."

Psalm 91 Summary

> Verse 1.) When we read our Bible and pray in our secret place, we are in God's presence and under His shadow.
>
> Verse 2.) The more we announce and praise the Lord for being our refuge and fortress and trust Him, the more confident we will be in His protection.
>
> Verse 3.) Be aware of the snares and pestilence being sent to you and who is sending them. Ask God for help, and trust Him for His deliverance.
>
> Verse 4.) Resting under the cover of God's feathers and having safety under His wing brings great comfort and peace. Knowing His truth is our shield brings security.

Verses 5 and 6.) Praise the Lord that He is in control and we do not need to be afraid of anything.

Verses 7 and 8.) When God pours out His wrath on the wicked for all their evil deeds, we can trust that it will not come near us. Rejoice that we are under His shadow and wing.

Verses 9 and 10.) Because we have trusted Christ Jesus as our savior and have made Him our shelter from trouble, we can rest assured that we are protected from evil and plague.

Verses 11 and 12.) Knowing that God's angels are taking charge of us and keeping us in all our ways gives great comfort, let us praise the Lord that the angels are picking us up and moving us to safety so we are protected.

Verse 13.) Be encouraged that we have been given the authority to put our adversaries under our feet. Rejoice that we are victorious!

Verse 14.) We need first to set our love upon the Lord, and then He will deliver us. Let us rejoice that God will set us up on high when we have a personal relationship with Him and know His name.

Verse 15 and 16.) Praise the Lord that He will answer us when we cry out to Him. Praise the Lord that He will deliver and honor us and give us a long life and His salvation.

Hallelujah, for His goodness and mercy shall follow us all the days of our lives (Psalm 23:6)!

CHAPTER 6

The Power of Wielding Psalm 91 in Prayer

God seeks intercessors who will stand in the gap and mediate for others. Ezekiel 22:30 states, "So I sought for a man among them who would make a wall, and stand in the gap before Me on behalf of the land, that I should not destroy it; but I found no one." Ezekiel 22:27–31 directly parallels what is happening in this day and age. I feature Psalm 91 as a prayer guide because every verse can be used in intercessory prayer and applied to any situation you may face. To make intercession is to pray or petition in favor of another. The following prayer is a rendition of personalizing Psalm 91 in a prayer format that you can use concerning your health, job, family, church, nation, government, or world. Use a firm voice to declare and decree the application of each verse. To declare means "to make known formally, officially, or explicitly." To decree means "to command." It says in Job 22:28, "You will also declare a thing, And it will be established for you; So light will shine on your ways." Pray directed to yourself or directed to someone else or a situation.

Psalm 91 Personalized Prayer

> Verse 1.) "He who dwells in the secret place of
> the Most High (El Elyon) shall abide under
> the shadow of the Almighty (El Shaddai)."
> LORD God, I ask You to bring me or
> _________ into Your secret place on high

to dwell with You. Bring Your shadow out around me, to keep me invisible, so the principalities, powers, rulers of the darkness of this age, and spiritual hosts of wickedness in the heavenly places are blinded to seeing me.

Verse 2.) "I will say of the LORD (Yahuah), 'He is my refuge and my fortress; My God (Elohiym), in Him I will trust.'" Thank You, LORD, for being my refuge and protection from _________ trouble. Thank You for being my fortress to protect me from outside forces or influences of _________. You are my God. In You, I will trust. Forgive me for not wholeheartedly trusting in You for _________ or in _________ situation. I ask You, LORD, to give me the ability to trust You for _________ or in _________ situation.

Verse 3.) "Surely He shall deliver you from the snare of the fowler, and from the perilous pestilence." I ask that You deliver me or _________ from the snare of the fowler, which is attempting to trap me in temptation and the sin of _________. I take the authority You have given me over the fowler and his snare of _________, and I tread it under my feet and command it to be rendered powerless.

I take the authority You have given me over the perilous pestilence of sickness, disease, and cancer. LORD God, I ask that You dismantle and remove all the energy, ionic charges, quark energy, frequencies, and the spirit of all cancer cells and organisms, such as viruses, flu, bacteria, parasites, spirochetes, or fungi that may be affecting me and render them powerless. Give me the ability to trust in the fulfillment of Your covenants and promises that I am healed by Your stripes and shed blood. I pray for the fulfillment of Romans 8:11, which states: "But if the Spirit of Him who raised Jesus from the dead dwells in you, He who raised Christ from the dead will also give life to your mortal bodies through His Spirit who dwells in you."

Verse 4–6.) "He shall cover you with His feathers, and under His wings you shall take refuge; His truth shall be your shield and buckler. You shall not be afraid of the terror by night, nor of the arrow that flies by day, Nor of the pestilence that walks in darkness, Nor of the destruction that lays waste at noonday." LORD God, I ask that You cover me or _________ with Your wing of protection and place Your feathers over me in all circumstances, to make me invisible and cloaked to those who want to afflict me. Thank You, LORD, for Your truth, the Bible, to be our shield and buckler. Cover me with Your shield of truth. May I hide behind it so all fear of the terror by night and arrow that flies by day will be deflected. I take authority over the pestilence of all organisms that walk in darkness to be neutered and made powerless. I take authority over the fear generated by evil men and women that it will be abolished. I look to You for my help.

Verse 7.) "A thousand may fall at your side, and ten thousand at your right hand; But it shall not come near you." LORD God, I ask that You bring Your wrath and vengeance on the wicked people behind the evil in this world so a thousand may fall at my side and ten thousand at my right hand, but it shall not come near me. You promised in Psalm 37:13 that their day is coming. I pray that You hasten that day. I ask that You fulfill Your covenants in Psalm 37 that the wicked will be no more. We will look for them, but we will not find them.

Verse 8.) "Only with your eyes shall you look, and see the reward of the wicked." Thank You, LORD, for fulfilling Your promise that I shall look and see the reward of the wicked with my eyes. Let the very net they have cast to destroy me or _________ catch themselves; into that same destruction, let them fall (Psalm 35:8). I pray that their swords of destruction turn back into their own hearts and that their bows causing death and destruction to be broken. I ask that the plots designed to destroy the righteous break and fail (Psalm 37:15).

Verse 9–10.) "Because you have made the LORD (Yahuah), who is my refuge, Even the Most High (El Elyon), your dwelling place, No evil shall befall you, nor shall any plague come near your dwelling." Because I made You my refuge and dwelling place, I am trusting You that no evil shall befall me or _________, nor any plague will come near my dwelling or in my body. I understand that I live in a wicked, fallen world that seeks to destroy me, so if plague and pestilence do make me ill, I ask, LORD God, that You would cover it with the blood of Jesus and release and remove it by the power of the Holy Spirit and in Your Son's, Jesus's, name.

Verse 11–12.) "For He shall give His angels charge over you, to keep you in all your ways. In their hands they shall bear you up, lest you dash your foot against a stone." I praise You, LORD, for giving Your angels charge over me to keep me in all my ways and to protect me from evil and all manner of pestilence. Thank You, LORD, for commissioning the angels to pick me up in their hands and bear me up above adversity lest I dash my foot against a stone or have harm come to me.

Verse 13.) "You shall tread upon the lion and the cobra, The young lion and the serpent you shall trample underfoot." Thank You, LORD, for giving me and all believers the authority to tread upon the lion and the cobra of destruction, and the young lion and the serpent of deception, we shall trample under our feet. I pray, LORD God, that You will keep me cloaked with Your feathers and shielded with the truth so the demonic and occult realms are blinded from seeing us.

Verse 14.) "Because he has set his love upon Me, therefore I will deliver him; I will set him on high, because he has known My name." LORD God, I have set my love on You. I ask You to deliver me from the plots, plans, pestilence, plagues, traps, snares, and all manner of evil set up for me by the wicked represented by principalities, powers, rulers of the darkness of this age, and spiritual hosts of wickedness in the heavenly places. LORD God, I know Your name. I ask You to set me on high so the devil who is going to and fro, seeking whom he may devour, will be thwarted from reaching me.

Verse 15–16.) "He shall call upon Me, and I will answer him; I will be with him in trouble; I will deliver him and honor him. With long life, I will satisfy him, and show him My salvation." Thank You, LORD, for answering my prayer when I call upon You. Thank You for being with me in times of trouble. Thank You for delivering me and honoring me. Thank You for satisfying me with a long life and showing me Your salvation. I ask for the fulfillment of this Psalm 91 prayer by the power of the Holy Spirit and in the name of Your Son, Jesus. Amen. I declare Isaiah 55:11, "So shall My word be that goes forth from My mouth; It shall not return to Me void, But it shall accomplish what I please, And it shall prosper in the thing for which I sent it."

This prayer is just an example of how to personalize Psalm 91. You can use this scripture and personalize it how you need it to fit your circumstance or situation. See addendum 3 for another example of praying Psalm 91, personalized against plots of the wicked and human trafficking. When I pray this deep and wide, standing in the gap, interceding for God's elect, I put the Bible on my head. I may also stand on the Bible to have that extra covering over me, under me, and through my prayer. It states in Psalm 119:105, "Your word is a lamp to my feet and a light to my path." This light does not allow the darkness to comprehend (John 1:5) what is being said or prayed. I do this to make my prayer invisible and cloaked. I like how the scripture in Romans 13:12 tells me to put on the "armor of light." Cloaking means to cover or hide so the demonic and occultic spirit realms do not know who to retaliate back on.

Retaliation

Early in my ministry, I suffered many retaliatory spiritual attacks when I prayed for people and situations. The demonic and occult realms do not like when you are treading on them or what they are doing. I asked the Holy Spirit to show me why I was suffering retaliation, and He gave me a vision of my prayer, acting like a pebble tossed into the pond, and the ripples went out. He told me that the demonic and occult realms could trace the ripples back to me and retaliate. The Holy Spirit also showed me a web weaving in the prayer grid system, and when a prayer went out, it would send out a vibration that would prompt a retaliatory attack. I would pray and ask God to bring in a fire and burn out this web. That was when I started to cover my head with the Bible. I have found that the King James Version and the New King James Version are the best cloaking versions.

When you stand on the Bible, take off your shoes and put a covering (e.g., a paper towel) between the floor and the Bible. I will anoint my head with the essential oil of frankincense because I have found that this oil is the best spiritual oil for protecting and detracting demonic and occultic spirits. I will ask God to stir up the firmaments so my prayers cannot be detected and traced.

Covering your head with a Jewish prayer shawl called a tallit is also beneficial. The word *tallit* does not appear in the Bible. It is likened to a garment with tassels on the corners written in Numbers 15:37–40 and Deuteronomy 22:12. A prayer called a "Tallit Benediction" came with my prayer shawl, and I was encouraged to read it before I put it on. It states, "Blessed art thou, O LORD, our God, King of the universe, who has sanctified us by thy commandments, and has commanded us to wrap ourselves in the tzitzit (seat-seat)." Tzitzit is another name for tallit.

There was a period of time when I struggled with retaliation as I went deeper into spiritual battle and intercession for this nation. One summer day in 2012, the Holy Spirit instructed me to get into the Bald Eagle Lake up to my neck. When I got in this disgusting, filthy water up to my neck, the Holy Spirit told me to integrate my energy into the lake water and then integrate the energy of the lake water into me. He said the demonic and occult realms will not see me. They will just see a lake. The level of retaliation attacks significantly subsided. When I need to do deep spiritual warfare and intercessory work, I get into my clean, warm water bathtub reservoir.

Spiritual Cloaking

I will bring in a spiritual cover or element cloaking to hide within when I go into spiritual-warfare sniping prayer mode. Sniping means to shoot (pray) at an exposed enemy from a concealed or cloaked location or position. I will pray in Romans 1:20, "For since the creation of the world His invisible attributes are clearly seen, being understood by the things that are made, even His eternal power and Godhead, so that they are without excuse." I will ask my LORD God to cloak me with His creation model and blueprint of the elements of the fire, air, water, earth, and living stones that He made so the evil spirits do not see me but clearly see only the elements, such as water. I will ask my LORD for the element sound (e.g., waterfall) to encrypt or conceal what I am saying or praying. Many people do not understand that all creation has a measurable vibration and a frequency, including stones, which is why Jesus said in Luke 19:40, "I tell you that if these should keep silent, the stones would immediately cry out." This verse tells me that God designed stones with purposed energy. First Peter 2:4–5 further states, "Coming to Him as to a living stone, rejected indeed by men, but chosen by God and precious. You also, as living stones, are being built up a spiritual house, a holy priesthood, to offer up spiritual sacrifices acceptable to God through Jesus Christ."

I was impressed with the cloaking of God's creation elements when I watched a scene in the *Lord of the Rings* movie where Frodo and Sam were trying to get to the gates of Mordor, and Sam got his leg stuck in the deep, loose stones. When Frodo was trying to get Sam unstuck, they caught the attention of the Orcs marching through the gates. As the Orcs approached Frodo and Sam, Frodo swung his brown cloak over him and Sam. In the eyes of the Orcs, they had just seen a giant boulder, and they turned and left. I liked this visualization of cloaking.

We can get inspiration from movies, books, nature, and our surroundings. For instance, my favorite hymn is "This Is My Father's World," and part of the second stanza states, "In the rustling grass I hear Him pass. He speaks to me everywhere." God is a part of all His created elements. This whole hymn blesses my soul and encourages my spirit, such as a part of the third stanza, which reads, "That though the wrong seems oft so strong, God is the Ruler yet." Hallelujah!

The following is a recap of all the means of cloaking and protection:

1) Seek to dwell and hide in the secret place of the Most High God—*El Elyon* (Psalm 91:1).
2) Abide/live under the LORD God's shadow (Psalm 91:1).
3) Get under the LORD God's wing and covered by His feathers—*Yehovah Rohi*: the Lord is my shepherd (Psalm 91:4). Run to Him!
4) Bring in the Truth/Bible to be a shield and buckler (Psalm 91:4).
5) Place the Bible on your head when you pray so it covers and shields your prayer (Psalm 91:4).
6) Declare the LORD God to be your refuge, which means protection or shelter—*Yehovah Machsi* (Psalm 91:2, 9).
7) If you have a prayer shawl (tallit), put that on your head.
8) Call on the angels to keep you and pick you up, thereby making you obscure (Psalm 91:11–12).
9) Set your love on the LORD God to then be placed on high so the enemy cannot reach you (Psalm 91:14).
10) Pray in God's invisible attribute of His creation elements to make you invisible—*Elohim* (Romans 1:20).

11) Anoint yourself with the essential oil of frankincense.
12) Hold onto the crucifix with your Bible.

Punch-in-a-Bag Prayer

When I have trouble discerning what is happening or feel blocked and do not know how to pray, I will pray what I call a "punch-in-a-bag prayer." I start throwing out and wielding what I call "revealing and striking scriptures" personalized, such as John 1:5, Mark 4:22, Luke 10:19, 2 Corinthians 10:4–5, Psalm 37:15, and Revelation 12:11. I start with putting frankincense oil on my head and then the NKJV Bible. This prayer may go something like this:

> LORD God, I ask that You punch in the power of Your Living Word and the fulfillment of Your covenants. Bring in the Shechinah glory light of You, LORD God, the light of Jesus Christ, and the light of the fire of the Holy Spirit so the darkness cannot comprehend. I command whatever is hiding to reveal itself and whatever is being done in secret to come into the light of the Triune.
>
> LORD God, I plead the blood of Jesus Christ over whatever is coming against me, and I ask for the power of Christ crucified to destroy the works and authority of satan. I ask You, Lord, to break all blocks, obstructions, and evil cloaking that are interfering with my ability to hear from the Holy Spirit and operate in my discernment. I bring in the power of Christ crucified and the shed blood of Jesus Christ of Nazareth, the Son of God, to intercept and obliterate the powers of the enemy coming against me. I put the divine bloodline between myself and the demonic and occult realms so they remain on the other side. I ask You, LORD, to bring in Your divinely commissioned angels to dismantle any

attachments, nets, webs, caging, podding, or foul spirit assigned to come against me and my discernment.

LORD God, I ask that You bring in Your divinely created elements of the fire, air, water, ground, and living stone frequencies and burn out, blow out, cleanse out, ground out, and spin out everything that is not of You and that is coming against me and blocking my prayer. I take the authority that You have given me to tread and trample on the serpents and scorpions of the enemy coming against me right now and to trample over all their power to render it powerless.

LORD God, I ask that You turn their swords back into their hearts and break their bows. I ask for every weapon mighty in You to take all strongholds, curse applications, and controls out of my spirit, soul, and mind. I ask this to be fulfilled by the power of the Holy Spirit and in the name of Your Son, Jesus. Amen.

This prayer is just an example. There are so many other scriptures that you can use.

CHAPTER 7

The Power of Discernment

This chapter teaches the reader to pray like a spiritual sniper. You will learn

- discerning precisely what your target and spiritual enemy are,
- how the enemy is coming against you,
- spiritual weapons you need before you go into prayer battle, and,
- specifically, scriptures you need to wield to have the most significant prayer effect.

Discernment means the quality of skill to determine what is hidden or obscure. We gain wisdom by reading and studying "the word of God, which is a discerner of the thoughts, and intents of the heart" (Hebrews 4:12). According to Hebrews 5:14, mature Christians "who by reason of use have their senses exercised to discern both good and evil." This scripture also implies that we develop skills in using God's Word for discernment, practicing, and applying the principles of God's Word to all of life. Proverbs 2:3 encourages believers "to cry out for discernment and lift up their voice for understanding." Proverbs 2:1–11 is filled with scripture on how to gain discernment. If you lack discernment, pray for it, believing to receive it (James 1:5).

Gift Assignment

We can pray for discernment, which is a gift from God. It says in 1 Corinthians 12:4, 10, and 11 that "there are diversities of gifts, but the same Spirit. To another the working of miracles, to another prophecy, to another discerning of spirits. But one and the same Spirit works all these things, distributing to each one individually as He wills." Spiritual gifts are given as God wills. It says in Ephesians 1:9, "Having made known to us the mystery of His will, according to His good pleasure which He purposed in Himself." The concept of God's will is not easy to understand, nor how He chooses to distribute these various gifts to believers. I pray you will be open to receiving the mystery of God's will and His spiritual gifts.

Why did God choose me to receive the spiritual gifts of discernment and healing? John 15:16 offers the best explanation. Jesus states, "You did not choose Me, but I chose you and appointed you that you should go and bear fruit, and that your fruit should remain, that whatever you ask the Father in My name He may give you." We need to ask for discernment. Another example of bearing fruit and receiving more from God is in the parable of the ten minas in Luke 19:12–26. Jesus says in Luke 19:17, "And he said to him, 'Well done, good servant; because you were faithful in a very little, have authority over ten cities." From this scripture, we can see that if we are fruitful and prosper in the little things first, God sees the nature of our heart and wills or gives us more.

Hearing the Voice of the Holy Spirit

I have been spiritually sensitive, discerning and hearing from the Holy Spirit for as long as I can remember. Reflecting on my days working on a head-injury rehab unit, I was sensitive to the unit's overall energy, whether or not we would have a good evening or if a patient was going to die. It is not something you can train someone to do. I think it is a part of how God designs people to be.

Hearing the voice of the Holy Spirit requires the gift of discernment and sensitivity to hearing His still, quiet voice. Through spiritual maturity and exercising my senses, I have developed the ability to have spiritual vision to see into many different situations and spiritual realms. Many biblical prophets were referred to as seers. In 1 Samuel 9:19, it says, "Samuel answered Saul and said, 'I am the seer. Go up before me to the high place, for you shall eat with me today; and tomorrow I will let you go and will tell you all that is in your heart.'"

Casting Lots Discernment Method

The act of discernment to get answers to yes-or-no questions was used throughout the Bible. In Exodus 28:30, Aaron wore devices called Urim and Thummim on his breastplate. The Urim and Thummim were sacred lots cast to obtain a yes-or-no answer to specific questions (see 1 Samuel 14:41–43). The disciples used the casting of lots to find a replacement for Judas. When I did a Bible search on casting lots, I found fourteen references. Gideon's "Sign of the Fleece" in Judges 6:36–40 was another example of a search for discernment and getting a yes-or-no answer. Gideon wanted to make sure that he had heard correctly from God. My friend Sandy wrote a testimony about how she and her husband used this fleece discernment method to help make a life-changing decision. You can read her testimony in addendum 1 after the last chapter.

Modern-Day Lean Discernment Method

In 1998, I learned a modern-day discernment method when reading *Stop Your Tinnitus* by Phyllis Avery. This book was about ringing in the ear. Halfway through the book, the author discussed food allergies as a possible cause of ear ringing. In one paragraph, she described how you could find out/discern if a food may be causing your ears to ring by naturally leaning forward or backward when you ask yes-or-no questions.

To do this modern-day lean discernment method to get answers to yes-or-no questions with the leaning method, stand with your feet neutral (shoulder-width apart) and your body weight evenly distributed over your legs. Then ask the question, "Which way is yes?" You will get a forward or backward lean. Then ask, "Which way is no?" This action establishes your discernment method to get answers to yes-or-no questions.

When I first read this concept, I was astonished at what I read. I went to my kitchen, grabbed sugar, and asked if it was good for me, and I leaned backward for no. I held another food item I knew was good for me and leaned forward for yes. I was amazed that it worked, and I have been teaching this discernment method ever since. You can practice by testing food, asking, "Are apples good for me?" If you get a bobble back and forth or sideways, that could mean a neutral answer, or you may need to ask more specific questions, such as, "Are peeled apples good for me?" If you do not get a lean one way or the other, try the finger-rub method.

Finger-Rub Discernment Method

I found that not everyone can do the lean discernment method. Another discernment method is to rub your thumb between your pointer and middle finger like the money sign. When you ask, "Which finger is yes?" your thumb will move to either the pointer or middle finger. Then ask, "Which finger is no?" Again, if you ask a question and your thumb stays in the middle, that means neutral or ask more specific questions.

There have been times I had previously established my ability to do both the lean and finger-rub methods of discernment and then cannot. When this happens, I will move to a different area away from cell phones, electromagnetic fields, or Wi-Fi energy. My inability to do the lean/finger discernment methods may be spiritual, so I will put my NKJV Bible on my head or hold it to my chest and ask, "In the name of Jesus, which way is yes?" Repeat for no. If this does not work, I will pray my "punch-in-the-bag prayer" to free myself to discern again. This prayer is in the last paragraph of the chapter on "The Power of Psalm 91."

Discovery and Gaining Knowledge

The lean/finger discernment methods are very valuable tools to assist you in discerning knowledge and making the decisions necessary to treat and deal with spiritual afflictions. It says in Hosea 4:5,

"My people are destroyed for lack of knowledge." This test helps you gain knowledge of a spiritual attack or why you are sick, what foods, herbs, vitamins, and products are good for you, if you need them, and how much you need of them to be well. It may also help you detect deficiencies, under- or overfunctioning organs, glands, and tissues, joint displacements, and food intolerances. These discernment methods work because your nervous system is "electrical" by nature and measures or senses the electron spin energy emitting from food or a product.

To understand electron spin energy, you need to know that everything on earth and in the universe has a specific molecular/electron configuration. Energy is produced when electrons move or spin around the nucleus of a molecule in a substance (e.g., food, herb, chemical, clothing, etc.). This energy can be positive or negative, and it causes weakness or strength in your body, which is measured by the lean/finger discernment methods. Likewise, you can discern what is happening in your body and how to correct it because your nervous system is connected to everything in your body.

God Connection

From a spiritual standpoint, the lean/finger discernment methods are very valuable tools to assist you in discerning knowledge and making decisions concerning spiritual matters. The following explains how this works: We are all connected to the LORD God by being a member of His body. First Corinthians 12:27 states, "Now you are the body of Christ, and members individually." Therefore, we are all connected spiritually through prayer. I visualize prayer and the spiritual connection like a grid system or matrix connected to everyone and everything, much like the nervous system in the body. In other words, God is the brain, connecting to all the members of His body through His spiritual nervous system, which I liken to a grid. Prayer energy is conducted through this grid of God's spiritual nervous system, reaching every member of His body.

Spiritual Discernment

You can use the lean/finger discernment methods spiritually to discern what we need to pray specifically and what scriptures we need to wield to have the most effective prayer. For example, you can use these discernment methods to find what scripture you need for a specific situation or discern what enemy is coming against you.

I use the scripture of Ephesians 6:12, "For we do not wrestle against flesh and blood, but against principalities, against powers, against the rulers of the darkness of this age, against spiritual hosts of wickedness in the heavenly places." If I discern a spiritual attack, I will use the lean/finger discernment method to establish the entity against which I am dealing. If I discern that I have an evil "power" coming against me, then I will discern what scripture I need to wield to get free from that attack. I will also use the lean/finger discernment methods to ensure that I first hear from the Holy Spirit and, second, hear correctly from the Holy Spirit. I will ask, "Is this truth in the name of Jesus and the blood of Christ?" I am amazed at how powerful this question is. Sometimes, when I ask "Is this truth?" I get a yes; but when I ask if this is truth evoking the name and blood of Christ Jesus, I get a no. I then clutch the Bible or gaze upon the open Bible or a picture/symbol of Christ crucified to discern further. First, I ask my LORD God to remove what interferes with and blocks my discernment. Second, I ask my LORD God to bring my discernment under His divine control so I may discern and hear correctly from Him.

Know Your Enemy

The Holy Spirit has imparted knowledge to me in greater detail concerning the four spiritual entities of Ephesians 6:12, which are the "principalities, powers, rulers of the darkness in this age, and spiritual hosts of wickedness in the heavenly places." I will refer to them in the rest of this book as the E6:12 entities. With this understanding, I have been more effective in doing spiritual warfare.

The "principalities" represent the satanic kingdom realm. The "powers" represent the occult realm. The "rulers of the darkness of this age" represent the wicked rulers, leaders, and elites who are "drawing the sword and have bent their bow, to cast down the poor and needy, to slay those who are of upright conduct" (Psalm 37:14) and who, "for without cause, have hidden their net for humanity in a pit, which they have dug without cause for our lives" (Psalm 35:7). They are controlled by the "principalities" and "powers." The "spiritual hosts of wickedness in the heavenly places" represent the alien/Nephilim realm. There are three places in Scripture addressing this representation. Genesis 6:2 states, "That the sons of God saw the daughters of men, that they were beautiful; and they took wives for themselves of all whom they chose." From this union came the giants/Nephilim, who were half spirit beings and half man. According to the book of Enoch, the Nephilim ushered in occult practices. Jude 1:6 clarified who the "sons of God" were. This passage states, "And the angels who did not keep their proper domain, but left their own abode, He has reserved in everlasting chains under darkness for the judgment of the great day." Paul alludes to alien entities in 2 Corinthians 10:5, where he says, "Every high thing that exalts itself against the knowledge of God."

Sniping Tactics

We can determine how we will pray and wield God's sword by identifying the specific tactics used by each of the four E6:12 entities.

The "principalities" (satanic kingdom) will use a direct physical attack on our health and mental status. I will pull my sword and strike with Luke 10:19, "Behold, I give you the authority to trample on serpents and scorpions, and over all the power of the enemy, and nothing shall by any means hurt you." Not all physical or mental issues are an attack. Use the lean/finger discernment method to determine if what is happening to you is physiological or spiritual. More information on deliverance techniques is given later in this chapter.

If a spiritual attack is coming from the "powers" (occult), then you will discern curses, hexes, vexes, black magic, spells, incantations, illusions, mirages, blocks, assignments, attachments, branding, graphing, alter controls, voodoo, etc.

I find that the "spiritual hosts of wickedness in the heavenly places" (alien/Nephilim) also operate similarly. They will use telepathic mind control (apparent communication from one mind to another by extrasensory means). If the spiritual attack comes from the powers or spiritual hosts, you will pull the sword scripture of 2 Corinthians 10:4–5. Personalize it and bring in all the spiritual weapons that are mighty in God to pull down all the strongholds (bonds, pods, matrixes, chains, yokes, etc.), cast down arguments (curses, hexes, vexes, incantations, etc.), and bind up every high thing that exalts itself against the knowledge of God, releasing all telepathic and controls on my mind outside of God's control, and command every thought to be brought into captivity to the obedience of Christ. Also, command all Nephilim ancestral corruption of your DNA to be bound, removed, and destroyed in the name of Jesus and by the power of the blood of Christ and Holy Spirit. I will often send it to the lake of fire and ask my LORD God to send His all-consuming fire through Nephilim pathways to destroy everything they are doing and that is not of Him. I may also send it to the lava and magma or lower parts of the earth as Psalm 63:9 states, "But those who seek my life, to destroy it, shall go into the lower parts of the earth." I put in an additional command to never return.

When I see that the "rulers of the darkness of this age" (wicked rulers, leaders, and elites) are operating, such as releasing bioweapons on humanity or any corresponding inoculations, I will unleash all the power of the LORD God's Word. I will wield whole chapters of God's sword, such as Psalm 37, 91, and 140; Psalm 35:1–8; and Luke 10:19. Particularly, Psalm 35:8 that says, "Let destruction come upon him unexpectedly, And let his net that he has hidden catch himself; Into that very destruction let him fall." I will also bring in Revelation 11:18. "The nations were angry, and Your wrath has come, And the time of the dead, that they should be judged, And that You should reward Your servants the prophets and the saints, And those who fear Your name, small and great, And should destroy those who destroy the earth [and your creation—people]." Lastly, I will pray Psalm 63:9–10, "But those who seek my life, to destroy it, shall go into the lower parts of the earth. They shall fall by the sword; They shall be a portion for jackals." See addendum 4 on "Declaration of Calamity on the Wicked."

Discernment Planning

After I have discerned what entity or entities I am dealing with, I will use scripture to discern how and what they are doing. For example, I will go through each verse of Psalm 91 one by one using either the lean/finger discernment method to make sure all of the verses of Psalm 91 are being applied. If I test no for verse 3, I know they are laying a snare or trap or causing sickness with a pestilence. You can use many other scriptures to discern what is happening and how to get set free and receive what you desire.

Next, I will discern what weapons I will need to do battle. For example, Do I need to put the Bible on my head? Stand on the Bible? Anoint myself with frankincense? View Christ crucified (addendum 7)? Play praise and worship music, Wholetones 852 Hz, the *Chant* by the Benedictine Monks of Santo Domingo De Silos, sacred music sung in Latin?

Then I will discern what specifically is being applied to me and wield Luke 10:19, taking authority over their plots, plans, and powers to use a snare, trap, or pestilence. If infirmity or pestilence is coming into my body, I will wield Romans 8:11, which says, "But if the Spirit of Him who raised Jesus from the dead dwells in you, He who raised Christ from the dead will also give life to your mortal bodies through His Spirit who dwells in you." I will also call on the Holy-Spirit scalpel, the double-edged sword of the Living Word of God, and the divine bloodline to separate and divide pestilence/sickness from my body.

Binding and Loosing

Our LORD God has given us the power to bind up the E6:12 entities and everything they do. Matthew 16:19 says, "And I will give you the keys of the kingdom of heaven, and whatever you bind on earth will be bound in heaven, and whatever you loose on earth will be loosed in heaven." The best explanation I have read concerning binding and loosing is in the book *Third Heaven Authority* by Mike Thompson. He states, "In the Greek text, the word translated 'bind' means to declare unlawful or lock away (bind up), and the word translated 'loose' means to declare lawful or to unlock (break)." The following is a general binding deliverance prayer. Fill in the blanks with what is manifesting.

> LORD God, I take the authority and power that You have given me to tread and trample on the serpents of _________ and scorpions of _________ and all their powers, to render them powerless. I ask You to bring in Your triune bonds of God the Father, God the Son, and God the Holy Spirit and bind up _________. I ask that You bring in the Holy-Spirit scalpel, the double-edged sword of Your Living Word, along with the power of Christ crucified and the shed blood of Your Son into _________ to root out and excise out _________. I ask that it be removed by Your divinely holy commissioned angels and be sent to _________, never to return from the beginning of time, end of time, and all dimensions, stratus, and direction of time. I also ask, LORD God, that You would bring down Your fire and burn out everything that is not of You and anything that gave permission for this spirit's presence. I ask this to be done by the power of the Holy Spirit and in the name of Your Son, Jesus. Amen.

Fill in the underlined areas with what you are discerning is coming against you. For example, the serpent could be a spirit of infirmity. The scorpion could be the symptoms manifesting. Bind up the spirit of infirmity and what symptoms are manifesting. Next, bring the Holy-Spirit scalpel, the double-edged sword of God's Word, and the blood of Christ into the _________ system and cells to root and excise out the spirit of infirmity and what germ/organism or cancer needs to be removed. Finally, send it all to the lower parts of the earth (lava and magma) (Psalm 63:9). You can also seek discernment to send these entities and devices to Sheol (Psalm 16:10), Hades (Revelation 20:13–14), fire (John 15:6), chains of darkness (Jude 6), and Jesus to be judged (John 5:22, 27). See the spiritual warfare prayer in addendum 5, written by Fr. Robert DeGrandis, SSJ, to learn how to have a more profound deliverance.

I will close with James 1:17, "Every good gift and every perfect gift is from above, and comes down from the Father of lights." I will name and loose what good or perfect gift I desire for God the Father of Light to impart, such as healing in whatever area of my body or mind. At the end of my prayer session, I will pray to put a spiritual wedge and barrier and a divine bloodline between _________ (i.e., E6:12 entities with their devices/tactics) and myself and my purpose, my destiny, my timeline, the steps God has ordered for me, and the race He has set out for me to run. I will apply Romans 1:20 to my spirit, mind, and whole being to be invisible and cloaked, making my voice, thoughts, and prayers cryptic and concealed to confuse the demonic and occult realm. Finally, I will ask the LORD God to rain down and loose His anointing to cover me and repel the E6:12 entities. These same prayer elements can be used to pray for others.

Summary of Spiritual Warfare

The following recap summarizes a spiritual-warfare strategy you can use to pray like a spiritual sniper:

- Discern precisely what your target is:

  E6:12 entities (Ephesians 6:12): principalities (satanic kingdom), powers (occult), rulers of the darkness of this age (wicked rulers, leaders, and elites), spiritual hosts of wickedness in the heavenly places (alien and Nephilim).

- Discern how the E6:12 entities are coming against you and if they are coming against many others:

   Principalities. Physical attack on health and mental status.

   Occult and spiritual hosts of wickedness in the heavenly places. Curses, hexes, vexes, black magic, spells, incantations, illusions, mirages, blocks, assignments, attachments, portals, branding, graphing, alter controls, voodoo, etc.

   Rulers of the darkness of this age (wicked rulers, leaders, and elites). Bioweapons that cause disease or sickness with corresponding inoculations.

- Discern what scripture is not being applied to you, your situation, and other situations.
- Go through each verse one by one of Psalm 91, Psalm 35:7, Psalm 37, 2 Corinthians 10:4–5, plus other scripture that speak of the work of the spiritual enemy.
- Identify what is not being applied to the situation or you.
- Observe what is physically or mentally happening: extreme fatigue and mental cloudiness, depression, and sudden pain/discomfort or nausea.
- Discern what cloaking you need to stay out of sight of the demonic and occult realms.
- Pray to ensure that the armor of God is fully intact and strong.
- Pray for the elements of God's creation (fire, air, water, earth, living stone) to cloak, encrypt, and not be seen or understood.
- Pray for Psalm 91:1, 2, 4, 11, and 14 to be applied and fulfilled.
- Cover your head and feet with the KJV or NKJV Bible.

- Cover your head with a prayer shawl (tallit).
- Discern what spiritual weapons you may need before you go into a prayer battle:

  > Need for the Bible to be put on the person needing prayer.
  >
  > Need for Bibles to be put on your head and under your feet.
  >
  > Need for frankincense anointing oil.
  >
  > Need to view Christ crucified (see addendum 7).
  >
  > Need to blow the shofar or ram's horn.
  >
  > Need to play worship music or Wholetones 852 Hz.
  >
  > Need to play the *Chant* by the Benedictine Monks of Santo Domingo De Silos.
  >
  > Need to ask for the holy, divinely commissioned angels to help (Psalm 91:11–12). Give them assignments.
  >
  > Need to call on the Holy-Spirit scalpel and the double-edged sword of the Living Word of God to separate and divide.
  >
  > Need to plead and speak in the blood of Jesus Christ.

- Discern precisely what scriptures you need to wield to have the most significant prayer effect: John 1:5, Mark 4:22, Luke 10:19, Matthew 18:18, 2 Corinthians 10:4–5, Psalm 35:1–8, Psalm 37, Psalm 91, Psalm 140, Isaiah 54:17, Revelation 11:18, etc.
- Discern what permitted the spiritual attack and what is needed to keep it from occurring again:

  > Confession of sin or negative emotion that may have permitted the attack: worry, fear, addictions, sexual immorality, etc.

- Remove and heal soul wounds and trauma. (See addendum 6.)
- Use the power of the Holy Spirit.
- Plead and speak in the blood of Jesus.
- Bring in the power of Christ crucified.
- Remove all negative thoughts and speech patterns and all possible permissions given for the attack.
- Remove negative claims, statements, and word curses (e.g., "I am not good enough," "I am sick," and "I am told I have three months to live").
- Remove wrong thinking (e.g., "I am worthless").
- Pray in James 1:17, explicitly asking God for the good and perfect gift you would like and need.
- Elements of deliverance or binding prayer:

> I take the authority and power that You have given me to tread and trample on the serpents ________ and scorpions ________ and all their powers to render them powerless.
>
> I ask You, LORD, to bring in Your triune bonds of God the Father, God the Son, and God the Holy Spirit and bind up ________.
>
> I ask that You bring in the Holy-Spirit scalpel, the double-edged sword of Your Living Word, the power of Christ crucified, and the power of the blood of Your Son into ________ to root out and excise out ________.
>
> I ask that it be removed by Your divinely, holy commissioned angels and be sent to ________, never to return from the beginning of time, end of time, and all dimensions, stratus, and direction of time.
>
> I also ask, LORD God, that You would bring down Your fire and burn out everything that is not of You and anything that permitted this spirit's presence.
>
> I ask this to be done by the power of the Holy Spirit and in the name of Your Son, Jesus. Amen.

The underline can be filled in by what you are discerning that needs to be prayed for or against. For example, the serpent could be a spirit of infirmity. The scorpion could be the symptoms manifesting. Bind up the spirit of infirmity and what symptoms are manifesting.

- Next, bring the Holy-Spirit scalpel, the double-edged sword of God's Word, the power of Christ crucified, and the blood of Jesus Christ into the _________ system and cells to root out and excise out the spirit of infirmity and what germ/organism or cancer needs to be removed.
- Finally, send it all to the lower parts of the earth (lava and magma) (Psalm 63:9). You can also seek discernment to send these entities and devices to Sheol (Psalm 16:10), Hades (Revelation 20:13–14), fire (John 15:6), chains of darkness (Jude 6), and Jesus to be judged (John 5:22, 27).

To get a more profound, extensive deliverance, see the spiritual warfare prayer by Fr. Robert DeGrandis, SSJ in addendum 5.

Keep Them Out

The following are steps to ensure deliverance and protection to keep evil spirits and demons from coming back and afflicting you:

1. Serve and trust God daily and have faith (Proverbs 3).
2. Obey the LORD God's Word (Bible).
3. Pray the prayer of protection:

LORD God, I ask You to cover *me/name* in faith
by the power of the shed blood of Your Son, Jesus.
I ask that You set a spiritual hedge of protection,
armor of light, and a bloodline around *me/name*
to protect *me/name* from the occult and demonic
attacks. I ask You, LORD, to fill *me/name* con-

tinually with Your Holy Spirit and presence. I ask that this prayer be fulfilled by the power of the Holy Spirit and in the name of Your Son, Jesus. Amen.

Also see Fr. Bob Hilz's prayer for protection and healing in addendum 5.

4.   Put the divine bloodline of Jesus Christ around you.

5.   Fill your mind with scripture and good thoughts (1 Corinthians 13:8 and Philippians 4:8).

6.   The satanic realm will attack and oppress you with negative thoughts that may influence you to behave and act badly. When negative thoughts or actions enter your mind—such as fear, worry, strife, offense, anger, complaining, etc.—it is important not to dwell on them or to yield to them; otherwise, you may open the door for an evil spirit or demon to afflict you. James 4:7 says, "Therefore submit to God. Resist the devil and he will flee from you."

7.   Find the appropriate scriptures that deal with your negative thought(s)/action(s) and meditate on them.

8.   If the negative thought(s) or action(s) have you held captive, and you are obsessing over it, pray:

LORD God, in the name of Your Son, Jesus, and by the power of the Holy Spirit, I ask that You inactivate and cover this thought/action of _________ with the blood of Jesus Christ. I command it to leave my thoughts and mind. I command it to no longer occupy my thoughts and mind or affect my emotions.

Pray 2 Corinthians 10:4–5. You may need to repeat this several times. Pray the prayer of protection.

9. Avoid temptations and sins that dishonor you and God, such as gluttony, pornography, gossip, slander, drunkenness, etc. (James 1:12–15).

10. Daily confess your sins and negative thoughts/actions to God, seek His forgiveness, and sin no more (1 John 1:5–10). Also, ask the LORD God to search your heart, expose, and root out sin patterns (Psalm 139:23–24).

11. If you sense a demonic/evil spirit attack, pray:

> LORD God, in the name of Your Son, Jesus, and by the power of the Holy Spirit, covered by the blood of Christ, I ask that You would inactivate and bind up the demonic force(s) that is (are) attacking or afflicting me or afflicting (name of the person). I plead and imprint the energy of the blood of Your Son, Jesus, into the demonic force(s). Remove them, and I ask You to commission Your angels to immediately take them to the courts of Heaven to Jesus Christ to be dealt with and judged. I command them never to return. Fill me (or the person prayed for) with Your presence and the deliverance power of the Holy Spirit. I ask that this prayer be fulfilled by the power of the Holy Spirit and in the name of Your Son, Jesus. Amen.

12. Pray Psalm 91, personalized as a deliverance prayer. If you need a deeper, more extensive deliverance and spiritual warfare prayer, see Fr. Robert DeGrandis, SSJ prayer in addendum 5.

CHAPTER 8

The Power of Discovery through Discernment

Many people have asked me, "How do I know that I am being spiritually afflicted?" The predominant symptom is profound fatigue, tiredness, and heaviness. People will tell me they feel their brain is shut down and cannot think clearly. If your brain is not functioning well, then nothing in your body will work well, and sickness will occur. Others have reported feeling agitated, depressed, foggy thinking, and having unexplained pain. When I am being spiritually afflicted, I often have cramping in my legs and back.

To discover what is causing your symptoms or sickness, use the lean/finger discernment method. Start by naming your symptom or illness and ask, "Why?" Is it physiological, nutritional, emotional, psychological, energy, spiritual, or a combination? Pay attention to words that pop up in your mind in your inner ear. Every morning and night, I discern if my brain is up and functioning; if not, I put the Bible on my head, discern why, and pray to fix it.

Physiological Cause

If you discern yes, that your symptoms are physiological, ask more questions. Discern what system or combination of systems is affected. Is it one of the following?

Neurological (brain/nerves)
Endocrine (glandular/hormonal)

Cardiovascular (heart/artery/veins)
Respiratory (lungs/bronchial/alveoli)
Lymphatic/immune (lymph nodes/vessels/thymus/spleen)
Gastrointestinal (mouth/esophagus/stomach/small and large intestines)
Liver/gallbladder
Pancreas
Kidneys/bladder
Reproductive (prostate/uterus/ovary)
Muscular/skeletal (muscles/bones/spine)
Connective tissue (skin/dermis/fat/ligaments/tendons/myofascial)

Get an anatomy and physiology book to help you answer the "why" question. Discern if any nutritional, emotional, energy, or spiritual factors may be affecting your physiological systems. A physiological issue often relates to infection, food, dehydration, supplement, medication, injury, inflammation, toxins, internalized emotion, stress, etc.

Emotional Cause

Discern if your symptoms or illness are related to emotional or psychological issues. Discern if it is emotional trauma or internalized emotions (bitterness, resentment, grudges, offenses, unforgiveness, anger, guilt, etc.). These emotions are sins that can attract spirit activity to further contribute to your physical, emotional, and psychological issues. Emotional trauma may also attract negative spirit activity that can further the effect of the trauma. Both emotional trauma and internalized emotional sin lead to soul wounds, which now permit the negative spirits to afflict you and form a soul contract with you. (See "Soul Wound Healing" in addendum 6.)

For example, the sin emotion of offense attracts the spirit of offense, which worsens your problem and may cause sickness. View the emotional trauma or sin emotion like a bird perch and the negative spirit like a bird. As long as the perch exists, the bird will want to land on it. The emotional trauma and sin emotion need to be bound, sealed, and removed. Use the following directed prayer to help identify and release emotional, psychological, ancestral, or spiritual causes of infirmity.

Directed Prayer

First, pray to bring in the light of Jesus Christ and declare that the darkness cannot comprehend. John 1:5 states, "And the light shines in the darkness, and the darkness did not comprehend it." Jesus is the light. He spoke in John 8:12, saying, "I am the light of the world." I will also bring in the Shechinah glory light of the LORD God (Adonai) and the light of the fire of the Holy Spirit. Shechinah means the dwelling of God, such as the cloud and fire that led the Israelites in the wilderness.

Second, command or decree that whatever is being hidden must be revealed, and whatever is being done in secret must come into the light of Jesus Christ. Mark 4:22 states, "For there is nothing hidden which will not be revealed, nor has anything been kept secret but that it should come to light." Viewing the Christ crucified picture in addendum 7 will be helpful in revealing any spiritual influence or affliction.

Third, pray and take the authority that Jesus Christ has given you over the emotional trauma or sin and the corresponding negative spirit(s). In Luke 10:19, Jesus states, "Behold, I give you the authority to trample on serpents and scorpions, and over all the power of the enemy, and nothing shall by any means hurt you."

Fourth, pray to bring in every weapon mighty in God (*Yehovah Tsaba*) to remove the emotional trauma, emotional strongholds, and soul wounds from word curse arguments that you spoke over yourself or spoken by someone else as stated in 2 Corinthians 10:4–5, "For the weapons of our warfare are not carnal but mighty in God for pulling down strongholds, casting down arguments and every high thing that exalts itself against the knowledge of God, bringing every thought into captivity to the obedience of Christ." Ask the LORD

God, in the name of Jesus, to remove and take the emotional trauma(s), stronghold(s), sin(s), soul wound(s), and all corresponding spirits and render them banished and powerless.

Fifth, pray to bring in what emotion you want or what healing you wish to receive. James 1:17 is a good model for this prayer, which states, "Every good gift and every perfect gift is from above, and comes down from the Father of lights, with whom there is no variation or shadow of turning." Name what perfect and good gift you want and bring in the light of the Father, our LORD, into your being and situation. Bringing in the fruit of the Spirit is a great start. Galatians 5:22–23 states, "But the fruit of the Spirit is love, joy, peace, longsuffering, kindness, goodness, faithfulness, gentleness, self-control."

Release, Remove, Barrier Prayer

Some people absorb other people's emotions and negativity, which is not good.

1) Recognize that you may be doing this, pray it out, and let it go.
2) Pray in what you want to see for that person, yourself, or your situation.
3) Pray to release any emotional or negative attachments. Be specific. Name it.
4) Put a spiritual, protective wedge and barrier between you and the other person or situation.

Command or decree that their negative emotion and energy are removed, grounded, and rendered ineffective. Grounding means to have the earth element absorb the negative energy, emotion, and stress. I often pray and ask God to open my spiritual alimentary canal and drain out the negative emotion, energy, and stress. The alimentary canal is another term for the gastrointestinal system, where food comes in and bowel content comes out. Spiritually, if negative comes in, then negative needs to go out. To bring in positive, feed on spiritually good things like reading your Bible, listening to praise and worship music, and studying and listening to Christian teaching.

In the book *Emotional Healing Made Simple* by Praying Medic, the author discusses situations we may find ourselves in that may trigger strong emotions. This may be related to a past trauma or a spirit manifestation. He defines a trigger as "a stimulus that sets in motion a programmed routine or reminds a person of some aspect of their traumatic past. A trigger may cause a panic attack, flashback, dissociation, or a switch" (p. 129). It is necessary to find the origin of the trigger using the directed prayer to remove what prompted the trigger. The author uses the following basic steps to heal simple emotional trauma (p. 36):

1. Recall an event from the past that causes a strong negative emotion when you think of it.
2. Identify the emotion(s) you feel.
3. Ask Jesus to take the emotion(s) from you.
4. Ask Him to heal the wound(s) in your soul.
5. Tell Him you receive His healing.

He continues, "If you are troubled by a negative emotion such as guilt, shame, or anger but cannot recall an event associated with it, omit step number one from the list. Simply identify the emotion you feel and give it to Jesus, then repeat as needed" (pp. 36–37).

Ancestral Affect

Discern if you have any ancestral emotional trauma, sin trauma, or sin emotions affecting you. These are a little harder to remove because they require deeper discernment. Some ancestral spirits reside in embedded compartments in our spirit and in ancestral iniquitous roots. Use the directed prayer format and apply in the scriptures of John 1:5 (light), Mark 4:22 (reveal), Luke 10:19 (trample), and 2 Corinthians 10:4–5 (pull down) to root out and remove the ancestral emotional trauma, soul wounds, soul contracts, demonic legal rights, sin trauma (e.g., murder), or sin emotions (e.g., anger) you may have gotten before birth. Cover all this with the blood of Christ and the power of the finished work of Christ's crucifixion on the cross to destroy and remove both the legal right and power of satan.

In my prayer, I will bring in the Holy-Spirit scalpel and the double-edged sword of the Living Word of God along with the power of Christ crucified and His blood to root out and remove patterns, cycles, imprints, grafting, scripting, programming, spirits, threads, cords, triggers, buttons, etc.

For example, my mother was an angry, rageful person, her mother was an angry, rageful person, and I have been and still can be an angry, rageful person. I refer to this as ancestral sin programming, scripting, or sin-set for anger and rage. It is an ancestral iniquitous root with a legal right for the demonic realm to afflict me. All ingrained ancestral sin-set patterns, programming, or scripting are at the cellular, spirit, soul, and mind levels. Cellular sin scripting is like music being etched into a vinyl record. Sin often occurs in sets of two, as stated in Romans 13:13, "Let us walk properly, as in the day, not in revelry and drunkenness, not in lewdness and lust, not in strife and envy." Other sin-sets can be binging and gluttony, addiction and lying, cheating and stealing, offense and unforgiveness, etc.

I recognize when the sin-set pattern of anger and rage is triggered, so I pray to break its pattern and remove its scripting and manifestation so I do not attract the spirit of anger and rage to make things worse. I also appeal to God as judge and Jesus as my advocate to remove the demonic legal right and corresponding iniquitous root of anger and rage along with any spirits and curse energy by the power of the Holy Spirit and in the name and blood of Jesus Christ. In Genesis chapter 4, God did not respect Cain's vegetable offering, and Cain became angry. God spoke to him in Genesis 4:7, saying, "Sin lies at the door. And its desire is for you, but you should rule over it." Sin is a spirit. Cain chose to open the door to the sin spirit of anger, which manifested into a rage, killing his brother Abel.

If I fail to rule over or take authority over the power of the sin spirit of anger, it becomes a willful sin leading to rage. If I do not repent, then I am in willful disobedience to the command of God to repent, seek forgiveness, and live honorably. If I remain disobedient, God will bring in a correction or chastening to prompt obedience to His commands. Proverbs 3:12 states, "For whom the Lord loves He corrects." Jesus says in Revelation 3:19, "As many as I love, I rebuke and chasten. Therefore be zealous and repent." If I fail to repent and bring my sin into subjection under God's authority and control, I will be disqualified from ministry, and I should not expect answers to prayer. Paul states in 1 Corinthians 9:27, "But I discipline my body and bring it into subjection, lest, when I have preached to others, I myself should become disqualified." To bring your body, emotion, appetite, addiction, sin, etc. into subjection means to have it placed under the authority or control of Father God, His Son, Jesus, and the Holy Spirit.

Spiritual Cause

Discern if there is a spiritual cause for your physical symptoms, mental shutdown, or foggy thinking. A lot of information about this subject is covered in the previous chapters. Other things to discern are whether the spiritual affliction is direct, indirect, remote, outside the body, inside the body, or through a person or people. Discern if the spiritual affliction may be coming from a device, curse, hex, vex, black magic, spell, ancestral spirits, roots, rootlets, branding, grafting, etc. Is the spirit realm using devices to create the affliction, such as darts, grips, hooks, lines, talons, arrows, wheels, spokes, hubs, coverings, plotting, rings, sabotage, blocks, interferences, attachments, co-attachments, marks, filaments, trailers, tentacles, etc.?

The list of what and how the demonic and occult spirit realm afflicts us is constantly changing. They are continually developing new plays and devices, so we are told to stay vigilant and pray earnestly. Colossians 4:2 states, "Continue earnestly in prayer, being vigilant in it with thanksgiving." Pray out the afflictions and devices and pray in the fulfillment of each verse of Psalm 91. Focus and meditate on being set free as written in John 8:36, "Therefore if the Son makes you free, you shall be free indeed."

The demonic and occult spirit realms will often retaliate to bring us back into captivity and under their control. Pray and ask the LORD God to bring confusion into these realms and take away all ability for them to communicate and to retaliate by the power of the Holy Spirit and in the name of His Son, Jesus. I will pray and ask the LORD God to stir up the firmaments so the demonic and occult realms have no idea where to retaliate.

Summary of Discovery

Discern if symptoms are a result of one of the following:

Physiological
- Neurological (brain/nerves)
- Endocrine (glandular/hormonal)
- Cardiovascular (heart/artery/veins)
- Respiratory (lungs/bronchial/alveoli)
- Lymphatic/immune (lymph nodes/vessels/thymus/spleen)
- Gastrointestinal (mouth/esophagus/stomach/small and large intestines)
- Liver/gallbladder
- Pancreas
- Kidneys/bladder
- Reproductive (prostate/uterus/ovary)
- Muscular/skeletal (muscles/bones/spine)
- Connective tissue (skin/dermis/fat/ligaments/tendons/myofascial)

Within these systems, discern if the issue is related to the following:

- Infection (virus, flu, bacteria, parasite, spirochete, or fungus)
- Food (sugar, dairy, pig, wheat, potatoes, etc.)
- Supplement (something you are taking or need)

Medication (side effects)
Injury
Inflammation (caused by sugar, wheat, etc.)
Toxins (environmental, occupational, metal, chemical, etc.)
Abnormal cell development
Internalized emotion or stress

Nutritional

Destructive food consumption (e.g., sugar, wheat, dairy)
Dehydration
Missing nutrient need

Emotional

Emotional trauma
Internalized emotions (bitterness, resentment, grudges, offenses, unforgiveness, anger, guilt, etc.)
Soul wounds
Soul contracts
Demonic legal rights
Emotions/negative absorbed from other people
A need for emotional deliverance
Recognizing that you need to pray it out and let it go
Praying in what you want to see for that person and yourself
Praying to release any emotional and negative attachments and putting a spiritual, protective wedge and barrier between you and the other person
Commanding the negative emotion and energy to be grounded
Decreeing that it can no longer affect you
Ancestral emotional trauma—generational sin-sets, patterns, programs, and iniquitous roots
Ancestral sin emotion
Spirit compartmentalization and roots

A need for deliverance from ancestral emotional trauma and sin emotion

Bring in the Holy-Spirit scalpel, the double-edged sword of the Living Word of God, and the power of Christ crucified and the power of the blood of Christ to root out and remove the following from all energy fields and cellular origins patterns:

> Imprints
> Grafting
> Scripting
> Programming
> Spirits
> Threads
> Cords
> Triggers
> Buttons
> Portals, etc.

Psychological
> Anxiety
> Delusions
> Depression, etc.

Energy
> Cell phones
> Satellite (location app left on multiple places in cell phones and tablets, SiriusXM radio, and navigation in cars)
> Electromagnetic fields (EMF) (electrical equipment and appliances, electric lines outside the house, dirty electricity from electric outlets, etc.)
> Radio frequencies (cell towers, digital electric meters, and cordless phones)
> Wi-Fi (routers)

Geopathic stress (underground lay lines and vortexes)

Spiritual
    Direct
    Indirect
    Remote
    Outside the body
    Inside the body
    Through a person or people
    From ancestry (mom's side, dad's side)

Comes in the form of the following:

    Curses
    Hexes
    Vexes
    Black magic
    Spells
    Ancestral spirits
    Compartmentalizations
    Roots
    Rootlets
    Branding
    Grafting, etc.

Devices used:

    Darts
    Grips
    Hooks
    Lines
    Talons
    Arrows
    Wheels
    Spokes
    Hubs

Coverings
Podding
Rings
Sabotage
Blocks
Interferences
Attachments
Co-attachments
Marks
Filaments
Trailers
Tentacles
Webs, etc.

ADDENDUM 1

Testimony 1
Rodney Fisher, MD

Pray with Purpose and Vision

When I traveled to Fargo for Micah's wrestling tournament, I got a high fever within an hour of arrival, and it lasted for eight days until a few hours before boarding the bus to come home. I prayed for relief from my fever every day, but only two days had meaningful reasons for me to be healthy. I needed to feel well the day Micah wrestled, and I needed to be well on the bus to keep from passing germs to the team. I felt well those two days only. Every prayer needs a worthy purpose. Mere relief from suffering is not a worthy purpose, as demonstrated by Jesus's prayer for "this cup to pass from me."

I recently healed a knee problem. It's the knee I had surgery on over thirty years ago. It recently began to lock up as if I was going to need surgery. I walked with a limp because I couldn't straighten it, and it was much worse during jujitsu. But I kept going. Anything I did with my knee, whether exercising or walking, I visualized myself doing it much better and many times faster. Physical pain can be feedback to let me know if I'm focusing or visualizing well. For example, I walk barefoot on gravel, imagining myself running very fast barefoot on gravel. If I lose focus, the pain immediately reminds me to refocus. The more I practice praying with purpose and vision, the more I realize that everything is a miracle and that miracles happen in the present moment, not just in the past or future; the power of visions is for the present moment.

Pray Positive

Prayer is the language of the universe. Positively spoken prayer has multiplying power and is much more powerful than negatively spoken prayer. Negatively spoken prayer also has power, but only additive power. They only add to your problems. A negative added to a negative does not create a positive, only a greater negative. Praying in negatives by using "no," "not," or "never" magnifies your problems. I didn't notice until I was sick at Fargo a few days later that many of the prayers were double negatives, such as "we come against disease" etc. Against and disease are negative words. My main point is that effective prayers are spoken in positive language or seen in positive visions for worthy goals.

Testimony 2
Karen O'Hearn

Psalm 91 has been a lifesaver for me! The power it has within its beautiful words is indescribable. I repeat it over and over until my situation changes for the better. Though it usually doesn't take more than once!

I recall shopping at Costco in Cave Creek, Arizona, parked next to a cart return near the tire garage. Upon returning to my car, I realized my gas tank had leaked all over the parking lot! The air reeked of gasoline, so I was afraid to start the car for fear of it blowing up, and I started praying no one would light a cigarette. I called AAA, and they informed me it would be one and a half hours until they could get there. They also would need to contact the fire department in case my car couldn't be towed. I then went to the Costco garage, and they couldn't do anything. No one was willing to help me. I started to panic and realized I would need to secure the area around me so it could be towed and to keep everyone safe. I put carts in the space in front of me for towing purposes, and a man started yelling at me and swearing, calling me names because he wanted to park there. He got out of his car and started moving the carts out of the way, not listening to my pleas. Things just kept getting worse, and short of crying, I got out my Bible app and started reading Psalm 91 aloud, putting myself in the text.

No sooner had I finished reading Psalm 91, a nice couple started trying to help me secure the area. Then, miraculously, AAA showed up an hour *early*! The nicest man got out and looked at the car, assessing things, and determined he could tow it without having to call the fire department. He recommended the best and least expensive place to tow it to for repair within walking distance of my home. Everything went smoothly from then on. Everything changed instantly after reading Psalm 91. Praise God for His protection!

Testimony 3
Sandy Foulkrod

Fleece Discernment Method

Harry (my husband) worked for a Silver Spring, Maryland, company. The headquarters of this company was in California. In the early 1970s, there was a huge cutback in the Defense Industry, and headquarters decided they would close the East Coast division for the good of the company. They invited all employees to move to California and offered financial aid to help with travel and expense. Harry and I talked at great length about moving. We made a list of pros and cons. Two big reasons not to go were our families living in Pennsylvania, and we had just moved into a brand-new house. Harry had been interviewing, but work for electrical engineers was very scarce. We had two weeks to decide, and one week was up. One evening, during our devotions, we read about Gideon putting out a fleece before God concerning saving Israel. Harry and I liked the idea and decided to put our possible move to California before God as a fleece.

With us, there were mixed emotions. We had four days left before we had to let the company know our decision to go or not. Our fleece was simple, "Lord, if we are to go to California, there will be no job offer. And if we are not to go, there will be a job offer before 5:00 p.m. Friday." We put that in a prayer and put it in God's hands. "Where do You want us, Lord?" Friday came and went—5:00 p.m., no job offer. So Harry committed to the transfer and signed all the necessary papers.

A phone call came on Monday morning, offering Harry a job close to home. A good salary and we wouldn't have to move from our newly built house. Because Harry was a man of integrity, he said he gave his word to move and wouldn't change it. So, California, here we come. We flew to California and bought a house. Our new house in Maryland sold quickly. Everything concerning the move went very smoothly. That gave us the assurance that we were where God wanted us, and we enjoyed the new adventures of the West. It turned out to be one of the best God experiences our family ever had. We were pleased that God had us move to California.

by Sandy Foulkrod

Encouragement
"I have...I can..."

Joel Osteen, pastor of Lakewood Church in Texas, has a confession for his congregation to say before Sunday service. The first four lines of the confession changed the way I read my Bible from then on. This confession states, "This is my Bible. I am what it says I am. I have what it says I have. I can do what it says I can do."

As I repeated the three lines, I determined in my heart that I would read my Bible with those three "*Is*." Reading the Bible this way has completely changed me as I'm learning "who I am in Christ," "what I have in Christ," and "what I can do in Christ." All scriptures are opening up to me. The promises are there all the time! I am now confident of God's love for me, what He has for me, and all I can do to advance my Father's work here on earth.

Confessions
"I have..."

I have the mind of Christ. "For who has the mind of the Lord that we may instruct Him? But we have the mind of Christ" (1 Corinthians 2:16 NKJV).

I have received the Spirit from God. "Now we have received, not the spirit of the world, but the spirit who is from God, that we might know the things that are freely given to us by God" (1 Corinthians 2:12 NKJV).

I have been bought with a price. "For you were bought at a price; therefore, glorify God in your body and your spirit, which are God's" (1 Corinthians 6:20 NKJV).

I have been crucified with Christ. "I have been crucified with Christ; it is no longer I who live, but Christ lives in me; and the life which I now live in the flesh I live by faith in the Son of God, who loved me and gave Himself for me" (Galatians 2:20 NKJV).

I have the ability of God in me. "Now to Him who is able to do exceedingly abundantly above all that we ask or think, according to the power that works in us" (Ephesians 3:20 NKJV).

I have all my needs met. "And my God shall supply all your need according to His riches in glory by Christ Jesus" (Philippians 4:19 NKJV).

I have been delivered. "He has delivered us from the power of darkness and conveyed us into the kingdom of the Son of His love" (Colossians 1:13 NKJV).

I have the love of God in me. "In this is love, not that we loved God, but that He loved us and sent His Son to be the propitiation for our sins. Beloved, if God so loved us, we also ought to love one another" (1 John 4:10–11 NKJV).

I have eternal life. "For God so loved the world that He gave His only begotten Son, that whoever believes in Him should not perish but have everlasting life" (John 3:16 NKJV).

I have obtained mercy. "Who once were not a people but are now the people of God, who had not obtained mercy, but now have obtained mercy" (1 Peter 2:10 NKJV).

I have God's sufficiency. "Not that we are sufficient of ourselves to think of anything as being from ourselves, but our sufficiency is from God" (2 Corinthians 3:5 NKJV).

Confessions
"I can…"

I can do all things. "I can do all things through Christ who strengthens me" (Philippians 4:13 NKJV).

I can come to the Father. "Jesus said to him, 'I am the way, the truth, and the life. No one comes to the Father except through Me'" (John 14:6 NKJV).

I can know Him. "That I may know Him and the power of His resurrection, and the fellowship of His sufferings, being conformed unto His death" (Philippians 3:10 NKJV).

I can be caught up. "Then we who are alive and remain shall be caught up together with them in the clouds to meet the Lord in the air. And thus we shall always be with the Lord" (1 Thessalonians 4:17 NKJV).

I can walk in the Spirit. "I say then: Walk in the Spirit and you shall not fulfill the lust of the flesh" (Galatians 5:16 NKJV).

I can rejoice always. "Rejoice always" (1 Thessalonians 5:16 NKJV).

I can fight the good fight. "Fight the good fight of faith, lay hold on eternal life, to which you were also called and have confessed the good confession in the presence of many witnesses" (1 Timothy 6:12 NKJV).

I can be healed. "But He was wounded for our transgressions, He was bruised for our iniquities; The chastisement for our peace was upon Him, And by His stripes we are healed" (Isaiah 53:5 NKJV).

I can move mountains. "For assuredly, I say to you, whoever says to this mountain, Be removed, and be cast into the sea, and does not doubt in his heart, but believes that those things he says will be done, he will have whatever he says" (Mark 11:23 NKJV).

I can be set free. "Therefore if the Son makes you free, you shall be free indeed" (John 8:36 NKJV).

ADDENDUM 3

by Janis M. Betz

Psalm 91 Personalized Prayer against Destruction by the Wicked

Verse 1. "He who dwells in the secret place of the Most High (El Elyon) shall abide under the shadow of the Almighty (El Shaddai)." LORD God, I ask You to bring me into Your secret place on high to dwell with You. Bring Your shadow out around me to keep me invisible so the principalities, powers, rulers of the darkness of this age, and spiritual hosts of wickedness in the heavenly places are blinded to seeing me.

Verse 2. "I will say of the LORD (Yahuah), 'He is my refuge and my fortress; My God (Elohiym), in Him I will trust.'" I will say to You, my LORD, that You are my refuge and my fortress. You are my God. In You, I will trust. Bring the people of this nation into a complete trust in You concerning what is going on and draw them to depend on You as their refuge and fortress, not the government.

Verse 3. "Surely He shall deliver you from the snare of the fowler, and from the perilous pestilence." I ask that You deliver us from the snare of the fowler, which is the evil of this government, and remove all traps laid for us to make us sick and disabled. I take the authority You have given me over the perilous pestilence such as the SARS-CoV-2 pestilence and crush it under my feet. LORD God, I ask that You dismantle and remove all the energy, ionic charges, frequencies, and the spirit of the pestilence from the SARS-CoV-2 organism and from all viruses, flu, bacteria, parasites, spirochete, or fungus that may be affecting us. Give us the ability to trust in the fulfillment of Your covenants and promises that You will keep us safe from any bioweapon pestilence and corresponding inoculation.

Verses 4–6. "He shall cover you with His feathers, and under His wings you shall take refuge; His truth shall be your shield and buckler. You shall not be afraid of the terror by night, nor of the arrow that flies by day, Nor of the pestilence that walks in darkness, Nor of the destruction that lays waste at noonday." LORD God, I ask that You cover us with Your wing of protection and place Your feathers over us in all circumstances to make us invisible and cloaked to those who want to destroy us. Thank You, LORD, for Your truth, the Bible, to be our shield and buckler. Cover the people of this nation with Your shield of truth. May we hide behind it so all fear of the terror by night and arrow that flies by day will be deflected. I take authority over the pestilence of all bioweapons that walk in darkness that they will be neutered and made powerless. I take authority over the fear generated by evil men and women that it will be abolished. I pray that the American people will look to You for their help. I take authority over the end game of the mass destruction of human life by any bioweapon or corresponding inoculation that it will not lay waste human lives at noonday.

Verse 7. "A thousand may fall at your side, and ten thousand at your right hand; But it shall not come near you." LORD God, I ask that You bring Your wrath and vengeance on the wicked people behind this bioweapon pestilence so a thousand may fall at our side and ten thousand at our right hand, but it shall not come near us. You promised in Psalm 37:13 that their day is coming. I pray that You hasten that day. I ask that You fulfill Your covenants in Psalm 37 that the wicked will be no more. We will look for them, but we will not find them.

Verse 8. "Only with your eyes shall you look, and see the reward of the wicked." Thank You, LORD, for fulfilling Your promise that we shall look and see the reward of the wicked with our eyes. Let the very net they have cast to destroy us catch themselves into that same destruction; let them fall (Psalm 35:8). I pray that their swords of destruction turn back into their own hearts and that their bows causing death to be broken. I ask that the plots designed to destroy the righteous break and fail (Psalm 37:15).

Verses 9–10. "Because you have made the LORD (Yahuah), who is my refuge, Even the Most High (El Elyon), your dwelling place, No evil shall befall you, nor shall any plague come near your dwelling." Because I made You my refuge and dwelling place, I trust You that no evil shall befall the Christians of this nation or me, nor any plague will come near our dwelling or in our body. I understand that we live in a wicked, fallen world that seeks to destroy us, so if plague and pestilence do make us ill, I ask, LORD God, that You would cover it with the blood of Jesus and release and remove it by the power of the Holy Spirit and in Your Son's, Jesus's, name.

Verses 11–12. "For He shall give His angels charge over you, to keep you in all your ways. In their hands they shall bear you up, lest you dash your foot against a stone." I praise You, LORD, for giving Your angels charge over all the believers and me to keep us in all our ways and to protect us from evil and all manner of bioweapon pestilence. Thank You, LORD, for commissioning the angels to pick us up in their hands and bear us up or lift us above adversity lest we dash our foot against a stone or have harm come to us.

Verse 13. "You shall tread upon the lion and the cobra, The young lion and the serpent you shall trample underfoot." Thank You, LORD, for giving me and all believers the authority to tread upon the lion and the cobra of destruction, and the young lion and the serpent of deception, we shall trample under our feet. I pray, LORD God, that You will keep us cloaked with Your feathers and shielded with the truth so the demonic and occult realms are blinded from seeing us.

Verse 14. "Because he has set his love upon Me, therefore I will deliver him; I will set him on high, because he has known My name." LORD God, I have set my love on You. I ask You to deliver me from the plots, plans, pestilence, plagues, traps, snares, and all manner of evil set up for me by the wicked, represented by principalities, powers, rulers of the darkness of this age, and spiritual hosts of wickedness in the heavenly places. LORD God, I know Your name. I ask You to set me on high so the devil who is going to and fro, seeking whom he may devour, will be thwarted from reaching me.

Verses 15–16. "He shall call upon Me, and I will answer him; I will be with him in trouble; I will deliver him and honor him. With long life, I will satisfy him, and show him My salvation." Thank You, LORD, for answering my prayer when I call upon You. Thank You for being with me in times of trouble. Thank You for delivering me and honoring me. Thank You for satisfying me with a long life and showing me Your salvation. I ask for the fulfillment of this Psalm 91 prayer by the power of the Holy Spirit and in the name of Your Son, Jesus. Amen. I declare Isaiah 55:11, "So shall My word be that goes forth from My mouth; It shall not return to Me void, But it shall accomplish what I please, And it shall prosper in the thing for which I sent it."

Psalm 91 Prayer Force against Human Trafficking by the Fierce Love 4 Good Team
Edited by Janis M. Betz

Verse 1. "He who dwells in the secret place of the Most High shall abide under the shadow of the Almighty."

LORD God, I ask You to bring every person held captive to human trafficking and their rescuers into Your secret place on high to dwell with You. Help them know that the secret place is within their being, not in some faraway place. Bring Your shadow around each captive and rescuer to keep them invisible so the principalities, powers, rulers of darkness of this age, and spiritual hosts of wickedness in the heavenly places are blinded to seeing them. May they know they are at last safe under the shadow of the Almighty and can trust in His all-powerful protection.

Verse 2. "I will say of the LORD, 'He is my refuge and my fortress; My God, in Him I will trust.'"

I will say of You, my LORD, that You are a refuge and a mighty fortress for all those held captive in darkness. May they know You are their God. May they know they can trust and depend on Your love despite their circumstances and surroundings.

Verse 3. "Surely He shall deliver you from the snare of the fowler, and from the perilous pestilence."

LORD God, I ask You to deliver Your children held in darkness from the snare of the fowler, the evil schemes of wicked men looking to profit from abusing and exploiting precious lives. I take authority over every dark and controlling entity that has come to destroy innocent lives and crush them and their evil agendas under my feet.

Verse 4. "He shall cover you with His feathers, and under His wings you shall take refuge; His truth shall be your shield and buckler."

LORD God, I ask that You cover Your children being held in darkness with Your feathers. Tuck them tightly under Your wings. May they rest and find refuge in Your comforting embrace. May Your children find freedom in coming to know the truth of You, Lord. I ask that the truth, found in Your Word, will be a mighty shield and protection from the enemy's schemes. I ask that You cover their rescuers with Your feathers and shield them during the rescue operations.

Verses 5–6. "You shall not be afraid of the terror by night, nor of the arrow that flies by day, Nor of the pestilence that walks in darkness, Nor of the destruction that lays waste at noonday."

LORD God, I ask You to replace all fear with Your perfect love. I ask that Your protection cover every captive each hour throughout the day and night. I ask Your Shechinah glory light to shine in the darkness, expose the terror, arrows, pestilence, and destruction, and render them powerless. LORD God, I ask that You put the armor of light around every captive and rescuer (Romans 13:12).

Verses 7–8. "A thousand may fall at your side, and ten thousand at your right hand; But it shall not come near you. Only with your eyes shall you look, and see the reward of the wicked."

LORD God, I ask that You bring Your wrath and vengeance upon the wicked exploiting and destroying Your children. May those held captive see a thousand fall at their side and ten thousand at their right hand. May it not come near them. I ask that only with their eyes they would see the reward of the wicked. Let the very destruction meant for the innocent fall upon the wicked. I ask that the sword of destruction be turned back into their own hearts and that their bows causing death be broken (Psalm 37:15).

Verses 9–10. "Because you have made the LORD, who is my refuge, Even the Most High, your dwelling place, No evil shall befall you, nor shall any plague come near your dwelling."

LORD God, I ask that You minister to the rescuers of the captives of human trafficking and the Psalm 91 prayer force intercessors. I ask that You be a refuge, keeping them safe from danger or trouble. Help them understand their need to keep You utmost in their life as You dwell in them to protect them from any evil or plague that might come near to do harm or sabotage their mission.

LORD God, I ask that those who have been held captive in human trafficking would make You their refuge and dwelling place. Help them to realize You can be trusted. I ask that You would cover them with the blood of Jesus. Thank You for getting them out of harm's way. Thank You, LORD, for always keeping Your promises. I stand on Your promise that You will never leave us nor forsake us.

Verses 11–12. "For He shall give His angels charge over you, to keep you in all your ways. In their hands they shall bear you up, lest you dash your foot against a stone."

Thank You, LORD God, for giving Your angels charge over each person experiencing the darkness of human trafficking, safeguarding them in all their ways, and attending to every need. Thank You for the safe escort Your angels are providing that not one precious child will dash their foot against a stone. I ask that You grant that no harm will come to them as Your angels hold them up and surround them. LORD God, I also ask that You cover the rescuers with Your feathers and bring the angels around them to protect and guide them and their rescue mission.

Verse 13. "You shall tread upon the lion and the cobra, The young lion and the serpent you shall trample underfoot."

Thank You, LORD, for giving us the authority to tread upon the lion and cobra of destruction, the young lion and the serpent of deception. I ask that You empower each captive being set free from trafficking to walk in Your authority that You have given them. Help them recognize the schemes and devices of the enemy meant to destroy and deceive so they may trample them under their feet.

Verse 14. "Because he has set his love upon Me, therefore I will deliver him; I will set him on high, because he has known My name."

LORD God, I ask that all those being trafficked come to know Your great name and set their love upon You. I ask that You will deliver them from the plots, plans, pestilence, plagues, traps, snares, and all manner of evil set up by the wicked who are representing principalities, powers, rulers of darkness of this age, and spiritual hosts of wickedness in the heavenly places (Ephesians 6:12). I ask that You set Your children high upon a spiritual mountaintop, out of range from attack.

Verse 15. "He shall call upon Me, and I will answer him; I will be with him in trouble; I will deliver him and honor him."

LORD God, please show every captive that they can call upon You, and as they call out to You, answers will come. I ask that they will come to know Your voice, feel Your presence, recognize Your honor for them, and make Yourself known to them in a very real way.

Verse 16. "With long life I will satisfy him, and show him My salvation."

I ask, LORD God, provider of everlasting life, that You will satisfy each captive suffering in darkness with long life. Please show them Your salvation. May they come to know their value and significance in You.

Thank You, LORD God, for Your power to deliver and honor every captive being set free. We ask and pray in agreement for the complete fulfillment of this Psalm 91 prayer by the power of the Holy Spirit in the name of Your Son, Jesus, applying His precious blood. Amen.

ADDENDUM 4

Declaration of Calamity on the Wicked

I wield Psalm 35:1–8 and Psalm 37 to declare calamity on the wicked as another form of spiritual warfare. These scriptures may be pluralized to include a specific group or be targeted to a particular person. Other scriptures that declare calamity on the wicked are Psalm 140, Psalm 63:9–10, and Ecclesiastes 8:13.

> Plead my cause, O LORD, with those who strive with me; fight against those who fight against me. Take hold of shield and buckler, and stand up for my help. Also draw out the spear, and stop those who pursue me. Say to my soul, "I am your salvation." Let those be put to shame and brought to dishonor who seek after my life; let those be turned back and brought to confusion Who plot my hurt. Let them be like chaff before the wind, and let the angel of the LORD chase them. Let their way be dark and slippery, and let the angel of the LORD pursue them. For without cause they have hidden their net for me in a pit, which they have dug without cause for my life. Let destruction come upon him unexpectedly, and let his net that he has hidden catch himself; into that very destruction let him fall. (Psalm 35:1–8)

Do not fret because of evildoers, nor be envious of the workers of iniquity. For they shall soon be cut down like the grass, and wither as the green herb. Trust in the LORD, and do good; dwell in the land, and feed on His faithfulness. Delight yourself also in the LORD, and He shall give you the desires of your heart. Commit your way to the LORD, trust also in Him, and He shall bring it to pass. He shall bring forth your righteousness as the light, and your justice as the noonday. Rest in the LORD, and wait patiently for Him; do not fret because of him who prospers in his way, because of the man who brings wicked schemes to pass. Cease from anger, and forsake wrath; Do not fret—it only causes harm. For evildoers shall be cut off; but those who wait on the LORD, they shall inherit the earth. For yet a little while and the wicked shall be no more; indeed, you will look carefully for his place, but it shall be no more. But the meek shall inherit the earth, and shall delight themselves in the abundance of peace. The wicked plots against the just, and gnashes at him with his teeth. The Lord laughs at him, for He sees that his day is coming. The wicked have drawn the sword and have bent their bow, to cast down the poor and needy, to slay those who are of upright conduct. Their sword shall enter their own heart, and their bows shall be broken. A little that a righteous man has is better than the riches of many wicked. For the arms of the wicked shall be broken, but the LORD upholds the righteous. The LORD knows the days of the upright, and their inheritance shall be forever. They shall not be ashamed in the evil time, and in the days of famine they shall be satisfied. But the wicked shall perish; and

the enemies of the LORD, like the splendor of
the meadows, shall vanish. Into smoke they shall
vanish away. The wicked borrows and does not
repay, but the righteous shows mercy and gives.
For those blessed by Him shall inherit the earth,
but those cursed by Him shall be cut off. The
steps of a good man are ordered by the LORD,
and He delights in his way. Though he fall, he
shall not be utterly cast down; for the LORD
upholds him with His hand. I have been young,
and now am old; yet I have not seen the righteous
forsaken, nor his descendants begging bread. He
is ever merciful, and lends; and his descendants
are blessed. Depart from evil, and do good; and
dwell forevermore. For the LORD loves justice,
and does not forsake His saints; they are pre-
served forever, but the descendants of the wicked
shall be cut off. The righteous shall inherit the
land, and dwell in it forever. The mouth of the
righteous speaks wisdom, and his tongue talks of
justice. The law of his God is in his heart; none
of his steps shall slide. The wicked watches the
righteous, and seeks to slay him. The LORD
will not leave him in his hand, nor condemn
him when he is judged. Wait on the LORD, and
keep His way, And He shall exalt you to inherit
the land; when the wicked are cut off, you shall
see it. I have seen the wicked in great power, and
spreading himself like a native green tree. Yet he
passed away, and behold, he was no more; indeed
I sought him, but he could not be found. Mark
the blameless man, and observe the upright; for
the future of that man is peace. But the trans-
gressors shall be destroyed together; The future
of the wicked shall be cut off. But the salvation
of the righteous is from the LORD; He is their

strength in the time of trouble. And the LORD shall help them and deliver them; He shall deliver them from the wicked, and save them, because they trust in Him. (Psalm 37)

ADDENDUM 5

Spiritual Warfare Prayer by Fr. Robert DeGrandis, SSJ
Modified by Janis M. Betz

> Heavenly Father, I love You, I praise You, and I worship You. I thank You for sending Your Son, Jesus, who won the victory over sin and death for my salvation. I thank You for sending Your Holy Spirit, who empowers, guides, and leads me into the fullness of life.
>
> Lord Jesus Christ, I place myself at the foot of Your cross and ask You to cover me with Your precious blood pouring forth from Your most sacred heart and holy wounds. Cleanse me, my Jesus, in the living water that flows from Your heart. I ask You to surround me, Lord Jesus, with Your holy light.
>
> Heavenly Father, let the healing waters of my baptism flow back through the maternal and paternal generations to purify my family line of satan and sin. In Jesus's holy name, I now reclaim any territory that was handed over to satan and place it under the lordship of Jesus Christ. I come before You, Father, and ask forgiveness for myself, my relatives, and my ancestors for any calling upon powers that set themselves up in opposition to You or that do not offer true honor to Jesus Christ.

Reveal

By the power of Your Holy Spirit, reveal to me, Father, any people I need to forgive and any areas of unconfessed sin. Reveal aspects of my life that are not pleasing to You, Father, ways that have given or could give satan a foothold in my life. Father, I give to You any unforgiveness; I give to You my sins; and I give to You all ways that satan has a hold of my life. Thank You, Father, for these revelations. Thank You for Your forgiveness and Your love.

Bind Elements

Lord Jesus, in Your holy name, I bind all evil spirits of the fire, air, water, ground, underground, and netherworld. In Jesus's name, I bind up any and all emissaries of the satanic headquarters. I claim the precious blood of Jesus on the fire, air, atmosphere, water, ground, and their fruits around us, the underground, and the netherworld below.

Heavenly Father, allow Your Son, Jesus, to come now with the Holy Spirit and the holy angels to protect me from all harm and to keep all evil spirits from taking revenge on me in any way. (And I put the divine bloodline of Jesus Christ between the evil spirits and me so they stay on the other side and are blinded [added by Janis M. Betz].)

Seal

(Repeat the following sentence three times: once in honor of the Father, once in honor of the Son, and once in honor of the Holy Spirit. [Fourth time in honor of the blood of Christ (added by Janis M. Betz).])

In the holy name of Jesus, I seal myself, my relatives, this room (place, home, church, car, plane, etc.), and all sources of supply in the precious blood of Jesus Christ.

Break and Dissolve

(To break and dissolve all satanic seals, repeat the following paragraph three times in honor of the Holy Trinity because satanic seals are placed three times to blaspheme the Holy Trinity.)

In the holy name of Jesus, I break and dissolve any and all curses, hexes, spells, snares, traps, lies, obstacles, deceptions, diversions, spiritual influences, evil wishes, evil desires, hereditary seals, known and unknown, and every dysfunction and disease from any source including my mistakes and sins. In Jesus's name, I sever the transmission of any and all satanic vows, pacts, spiritual bonds, soul ties, and satanic works. In Jesus's name, I break and dissolve any and all links and effects of links with astrologers, bohmos, channelers, charters, clairvoyants, crystal healers, crystals, fortune tellers, mediums, the New Age Movement, occult seers, palm, tea leaf, or tarot-card readers, psychics, santeros, satanic cults, spirit guide, witches, witchdoctors, and voodoo. In Jesus's name, I dissolve all effects of participation in seances and divination, Ouija boards, horoscopes, occult games of all sorts, and any form of worship that does not offer true honor to Jesus Christ.

Post Deliverance Clearing

Holy Spirit, please reveal to me through word of knowledge any evil spirits that have attached themselves to me in any way. (Pause and wait for words to come to you, such as anger, arrogance, bitterness, brutality, confusion, cruelty, deception, envy, fear, hatred, insecurity, jealousy, pride, resentment, or terror. Pray the following for each of the evil spirits revealed.)

In the name of Jesus, I rebuke you spirit of __________. I command you to go directly to Jesus, without manifestation and harm to me or anyone, so He can dispose of you according to His holy will.

I thank You, Heavenly Father, for Your love. I thank You, Holy Spirit, for empowering me to be aggressive against satan and evil spirits. I thank You, Jesus, for setting me free.

Lord Jesus, fill me with charity, compassion, faith, gentleness, hope, humility, joy, kindness, light, love, mercy, modesty, patience, please, purity, security, serenity, tranquility, trust, truth, understanding, and wisdom. Help me walk in Your light and truth, illuminated by the Holy Spirit so, together, we may praise, honor, and glorify our Father in time and eternity. For You, Lord Jesus, are "the way, the truth, and the life" (John 14:6), and You "have come that we might have life and have it more abundantly" (John 10:10).

"God indeed is my savior; I am confident and unafraid. My strength and courage is the Lord, and He has been my savior" (Isaiah 12:2). Amen.

Protection and Healing Prayer by Fr. Bob Hilz
Modified by Janis M. Betz

Most High and Glorious God: Father, Son, and Holy Spirit, I praise, worship, adore, and thank

You for who You are and all You have given me, and I ask forgiveness for all my sins. Please cover me with the healing, protective, precious blood of Jesus Christ (Colossians 1:20) and give me all the graces I need to live Your abundant life today (John 10:10).

Holy Spirit, please remove all blocks in me to receiving and sharing Your love and grace. Heal all my wounds and negative emotions, all negative genetic, intergenerational, addictive, compulsive, conscious, and subconscious and unconscious material: past, present, and to come, known and unknown, against me, my relationships and family, finances and possessions, ministry, electronic and computer work, and all my transportation vehicles.

I ask forgiveness of my own body for not taking care of it, and I forgive its negative reactions to me and remove all tension, stress, fear, and worry. I ask forgiveness from all those whom I have injured, and I forgive all who have injured me (Matthew 6:14–15). May my whole person be healed and transformed (Romans 12:2) by the Holy Spirit (Acts 1:8).

In the name of God the Father, Son, and Holy Spirit, I bind and break the commands of ruling spirits to harm us (1 Peter 5:8–9) in all ways and for all purposes in my mind, in the fire, air, atmosphere, wind, water, ground, underground, the satanic forces of nature, and all communication media. I render their orders null and void, leaving no area where any negative forces, spirits, and all their emissaries can get to me (or us, for our families).

To all of these spirits, I command you in the name of the Father, the Son, and the Holy

Spirit, to leave us without doing any harm and go peacefully and quietly, immediately to Jesus Christ to be judged (John 5:22, 27) and never return to harm us again. Jesus, please heal the effects of these spirits in and around us.

Dear Holy Spirit, please fill me up (Romans 5:5) to overflowing with all You have for me today and set me totally on fire with Your all-consuming and purifying love so I may be Your light and blessing in the world today. All this, Father, I pray in the name of Your Son, Jesus, and the Holy Spirit. Amen.

People in ministry are under a different kind of attack. Witches send stuff at us three times to mock the Holy Trinity. Pray in the name of each member of the Holy Trinity: "Father, remove all satanic things around and thrown at me and send back to them your graces of faith, conversion, and repentance." Pray again in the names of Christ Jesus and the Holy Spirit.

We are all temples of God (1 Corinthians 6:19) in spiritual combat (1 Peter 5:6–9) needing spiritual clothes (Ephesians 6:10–20), yet we all have victory with Jesus Christ (Revelation 7:14) in the power of the Holy Spirit (Acts 1:8).

Soul Wound Healing

by Katie Souza from *The Healing School* CD Set
Edited by Janis M. Betz

Introduction to Soul Wounds
Foundation of the soul:

- Mind
- Will
- Emotion

When you become a Christian, your spirit instantly connects to the spirit of Jesus Christ. His shed blood redeemed and cleansed your spirit from sin, but your soul goes through a process of healing.

Sin-created wounds and emotional trauma wounds may still mark your soul.

What Do Soul Wounds Do?
Soul wounds affect and control the following:

- Peace level
- Thought process
- Will (right versus wrong)
- Emotions
- Relationships
- Level of dominion over demonic powers
- Financial increase

"My soul loathes my life; I will give free course to my complaint, I will speak in the bitterness of my soul" (Job 10:1).

How Are Soul Wounds Created?

Soul wounds are created by sin and emotional or spiritual trauma.

- By others' sin against you (rejection, anger, hurtful words, abuse).
- By your sin against yourself (adultery, pornography, drugs, lying, not forgiving).
- Editor's note: *Soul wounds may also be imprinted ancestral sin(s) passed down from generation to generation. You can have ancestral soul wounds imprinted on your soul and have soul contracts that need to be broken.*

Soul wounds create more sin and stimulate you to sin even more.

- "For the good that I will to do, I do not do; but the evil I will not to do, that I practice. Now if I do what I will not to do, it is no longer I who do it, but sin that dwells in me" (Romans 7:19–20).
- Against your intentions, you will continue to sin until the soul wound is healed.
- The healing of a soul wound will cause the sin associated with that wound to cease.

How Do Soul Wounds Work?

Because soul wounds are created by sin, it gives the demonic the legal right to torment you. The demonic can operate through unhealed soul wounds. Sin is an open door for the enemy.

- "For the enemy has persecuted my soul; He has crushed my life to the ground; He has made me dwell in darkness, Like those who have long been dead" (Psalm 143:3–4).

    - You can rebuke the enemy repeatedly and do deliverance, but until the soul wound is dealt with, the demonic will have access, and you will continue to struggle with sin.

- "I will no longer talk much with you, for the ruler of this world is coming, and he has nothing in Me" (John 14:30).

    - Jesus had nothing in common with the demonic, so they had no power over Him.
    - Our sin gives us common ground with the demonic, allowing them dominion over us.

- "Then they came to the other side of the sea, to the country of the Gadarenes. And when He had come out of the boat, immediately there met Him out of the tombs a man with an unclean spirit, who had his dwelling among the tombs; and no one could bind him, not even with chains" (Mark 5:1–3).

    - In this passage, a man wandered "the tombs." The word "tomb" means "to recall or remember" or a "monument" set up as a constant remembrance of what happened to you years ago with corresponding negative emotions. A soul wound is a monument set up to control you constantly. This passage shows how the demonic can trap you in your sinful ways, but Jesus (Christ crucified) has the power to overpower the demonic realm. Sin often manifests from soul wounds, which permit the demonic realm to afflict you and keep you in the sin pattern.

Soul wounds can affect both bodily health and financial prosperity.

- "Beloved, I pray that you may prosper in all things and be in health, just as your soul prospers" (3 John 2).

  - You may not have financial blessings when your soul is wounded because the blessings would not be used properly.
  - The soul must prosper for the blessing to prosper as God intends because your will would be under the control of the soul wound instead of the desire of God.
  - Bodily health is connected to the soul's health because the demonic can access you through a soul wound.
  - The demonic can torment you (with disease and infirmity) because of soul wounds.

How Are Soul Wounds Healed?

Soul wounds can be healed by the supernatural tool: "the glory light of Jesus."

Editor's note: *Soul wounds may also be healed by the power of Christ crucified and the shed blood of Jesus Christ (Yeshua Ha'Mashiach).*

You can command the demonic to leave, but until the wound that allowed them access is healed (and all subsequent wounds), they can return and create further affliction.

  - "Therefore lay aside all filthiness and overflow of wickedness, and receive with meekness the implanted word, which is able to save your souls" (James 1:21). The Word of God can heal soul wounds.
  - "Then Jesus spoke to them again, saying, 'I am the light of the world. He who follows Me shall not walk in darkness, but have the light of life'" (John 8:12). Jesus is the "light of the world" (refers to the soul).

- "I have come as a light into the world, that whoever believes in Me should not abide in darkness" (John 12:46). This passage refers not only to the darkness of the world but also to the darkness of our souls.

- "The lamp of the body is the eye. Therefore, when your eye is good, your whole body also is full of light. But when your eye is bad, your body also is full of darkness. Therefore take heed that the light which is in you is not darkness. If then your whole body is full of light, having no part dark, the whole body will be full of light, as when the bright shining of a lamp gives you light" (Luke 11: 34–36). The eye is referred to as the window into the soul. If you have soul wounds, your body can easily be filled with darkness.

- "There is no soundness in my flesh Because of Your anger, Nor any health in my bones Because of my sin. For my iniquities have gone over my head; Like a heavy burden they are too heavy for me. My wounds are foul and festering Because of my foolishness. I am troubled, I am bowed down greatly; I go mourning all the day long. For my loins are full of inflammation, And there is no soundness in my flesh. I am feeble and severely broken; I groan because of the turmoil of my heart. Lord, all my desire is before You; And my sighing is not hidden from You. My heart pants, my strength fails me; As for the light of my eyes, it also has gone from me" (Psalm 38:3–10). Sin creates soul wounds and then weakness in the body and health.

Steps to Heal a Soul Wound

1. Have a focused amount of time on repentance and forgiveness. Editor's note: *Also, take time to lament the cause of your*

soul wound. To lament *means "to express sorrow, mourning, or regret strongly."*

a.   Do not use overview (generalize) references.

b.   Whether someone else's sin created the soul wound (e.g., hate or rejection expressed toward you) or your sin resulted in the soul wound (e.g., hate or not forgiving yourself), you need to seek repentance for those sins.

c.   Forgiveness must be given to others for the soul to be healed. No matter the severity of the sin, this is for your health, joy, peace, love, etc.

2.   Soak your soul in the glory light of Jesus.

d.   Use faith to believe what the scriptures say:

i.   That the light of Jesus causes your soul to be healed.

e.   "Then they journeyed from Mount Hoor by the Way of the Red Sea, to go around the land of Edom; and the soul of the people became very discouraged on the way. And the people spoke against God and against Moses: 'Why have you brought us up out of Egypt to die in the wilderness? For there is no food and no water, and our soul loathes this worthless bread.' So the LORD sent fiery serpents among the people, and they bit the people; and many of the people of Israel died. Therefore the people came to Moses, and said, 'We have sinned, for we have spoken against the LORD and against you; pray to the LORD that He take away the serpents from us.' So Moses prayed for the people. Then the LORD said to Moses, 'Make a fiery serpent, and set it on a pole; and it shall be that everyone who is bitten, when he looks at it, shall live.' So Moses made a bronze serpent, and put it on a pole; and so it was, if a serpent had bitten anyone, when he looked at the bronze serpent, he lived" (Numbers 21:4–9).

    i.   This is an example of how focusing on the glory light of Jesus can heal soul wounds.

    ii.   The Israelites' complaining created soul wounds that could only be healed through an attentive focus on the bronze serpent. Editor's note: *Likewise, focusing on Christ crucified, hanging on the cross brings deliverance and healing. See addendum 7.*

    iii.   Referenced in John 3:14–15: "And as Moses lifted up the serpent in the wilderness, even so must the Son of Man be lifted up, that whoever believes in Him should not perish but have eternal life." Editor's note: Moses's pole with the serpent lifted up was a banner that brought victory over death. Likewise, Jesus Christ lifted up on the cross is a banner that brings deliverance, healing, and victory over satan's power of death (*Yehovah Nissi*: the LORD is my banner).

f.   Attentively focus on Jesus's glory light.

    i.   Avoid becoming distracted—meditate on scripture.

    ii.   Avoid force-seeing the glory light by overimagining it.

g.   Soak in the glory light for fifteen minutes before bed because it will help bring about revelations.

3.   Pay attention to visions and dreams. Put paper and a pencil next to the bed to record dreams.

h.   Soak in the glory light after visions and dreams have been revealed about wounds.

"In a dream, in a vision of the night, When deep sleep falls upon men, While slumbering on their beds, then He opens the ears of men, And seals their instruction. In order to turn man from his deed, And conceal pride from man, He keeps back his soul from the Pit, And his life from perishing by the sword" (Job 33:15–18).

    i.   Focus on the revealed information.

  i.   Allow God to determine the order in which you address your wounds.

    i.   Let the light show you, and don't rush revelations.

4.   Don't allow yourself to get bothered, troubled, or depressed by dream revelations.

  j.   Take your focus off your soul wound/event and focus on the glory light of Jesus healing your soul wounds.

5.   Expect God to reveal unhealthy "soul ties."

  k.   A soul tie links souls between two people together, as well as your mind, will, and emotions. That is why it is hard to let go of someone.

    i.   A positive soul tie is a godly marriage that unites the soul.

    ii.   A negative soul tie is created through sin (e.g., fornication, premarital sex, adultery, molestation, or rape).

6.   Soak until you receive confirmation that a particular wound is healed.

  l.   Confirmation can come from confidence in your faith that the soul wound is gone, scriptural assurance given by the Holy Spirit, and a sense of peace.

m. Confirmation may also come from revelation, dreams, and visions.

    i. "The peace of God, which surpasses all understanding, will guard your hearts and minds through Christ Jesus" (Philippians 4:7).

7. Once a wound is healed, you can command the demonic part to leave.

n. While the wounds are being healed, the demonic and occult realms will attempt to discourage your efforts.

o. Editor's note: *Bring in the healing power of the shed blood of Jesus Christ into your sin and soul. Bring in the power of Christ crucified to destroy any demonic right to afflict.*

8. Soak your soul in worship.

p. God's glory encompasses praise.

q. It ensures continued soul health.

Testimony of a Healed Soul Wound

A friend had given me this CD set about twelve years ago, and I took it to the beach and listened to them. It ministered to my soul so powerfully that I cried and prayed. The Holy Spirit revealed many wounds that needed healing and people I needed to forgive. These wounds came from many generations of ancestral sins and emotional traumas. Many wounds were also caused by not only my trauma events that occurred in my own life but also in my ancestry. It took me a while to unlayer them all. The Holy Spirit said that the demonic and occult spirit realm still had permission to access me through a soul wound I had inflicted on my mother. My mother and I fought a lot when I was a teenager, and I often verbalized my hate for her. I asked my mother to forgive me, and she said, "Oh, you were just being a teenager." I took that as forgiveness and asked God to heal the soul wound I gave her. The most freeing act of obedience was to write a forgiveness letter to my mother. That was very hard to do, but it lifted a weight off me and provided healing for my soul.

ADDENDUM 7

Christ Crucified

Figure 1

On January 19, 2023, I was praying with a client with a strong family history of occult activity. I had difficulty detaching an attachment from his soul. This attachment was an avenue for occult spirit activity to keep him ill. The Holy Spirit instructed me to have him look at the Christ crucified hanging on the wall. I brought in the glory light of Jesus Christ, and the occult attachment on his soul lifted off. I brought in the blood of Jesus Christ to cover his soul and release his infirmities, and the physical manifestation lifted.

Redeemer's Love with Crosses

Figure 2
Painting by Venessa Hurabuena (venessahurabuena.com)

I encourage you to purchase this print of Redeemer's Love with Crosses to help you with discernment, deliverance, and healing work.

Venessa is a prophetic painter, and the Holy Spirit inspired her to paint this painting. It holds a vibration that has helped me in my deliverance and healing sessions. The Holy Spirit revealed to me that any spiritual activity that is present will be made known when I view Christ crucified and encourage my clients to do the same.

REFERENCES

1977. New American Standard (NAS) Bible. LaHabra: The Lockman Foundation.

1982. The New King James Version (NKJV) Bible. Nashville: Thomas Nelson.

1984. New International Version (NIV) Bible. Grand Rapids: Zonderva.

1985. The Interlinear Bible. Peabody: Hendrickson.

1993. *Compact Bible Dictionary*. Grand Rapids: Zonderva.

2001. English Standard Version (ESV) Bible. Wheaton: Crossway.

2013. Cepher. Everett: Cepher Publishing Group.

2016. The Complete Jewish Study Bible. Peabody: Hendrickson.

Emoto, Masaru. 2001. *The Hidden Messages in Water*. Beyond Words.

Evans, Tony. 2014. *The Power of God's Names*. Harvest House Publishers.

King James Version (KJV) Bible. Iowa Falls: World Bible Publishers.

Medic, Praying. 2023. *Emotional Healing Made Simple*. Inkity Press.

Ruth, P. J, and A. R. Schum. 2009. *Psalm 91: Real-Life Stories of God's Shield of Protection*. Better Living Ministries.

The Merriam-Webster's Collegiate Dictionary, 11th ed.

Thompson, Mike. 2023. *Third Heaven Authority*. Charisma House.

Whyte, H. A. Maxwell. 2005. *The Power of the Blood*. Whitaker House.

SCRIPTURE INDEX

Abide in Christ
  John 15:6 38
Angels left their abode
  Jude 1:6 71
Anxious
  Philippians 4:6-7 31
Armor of God
  Ephesians 6:13-17 1
Armor of light
  Romans 13:12-14 33
Ask and not receive
  James 4:3 36
Ask in Jesus's name
  John 15:16 25
Authority
  Luke 10:19 4, 15
Bind and loose
  Matthew 16:19 73
Blessing and cursing
  James 3:10 3
Blood cleansing your conscience
  Hebrews 9:14 19
Blood is the Life
  Leviticus 17:11 23
Blood of Jesus
  1 John 1:7 19
Blood of sprinkling
  Hebrews 12:24 21
Blood of the Lamb
  Revelations 12:11 20
Body of Christ
  1 Corinthians 12:27 69
Chosen by God
  John 15:16 66

Christ died for us
  Romans 5:8 39
Christ's death destroyed satan's power
  Hebrews 2:14-15 20
Cloak with elements
  Romans 1:20 60
Confess and believe
  Romans 10:9 39
Correction
  Proverbs 3:12 89
Declare
  Job 22:28 53
Deliver from evil
  2 Timothy 4:18 47
Destroy life
  Psalm 63:9 72
Destroy the wicked
  Psalm 35:8 72
Devil like a lion
  1 Peter 5:8 49
Devil-resist-flee
  James 4:7 80
Devil's snare
  2 Timothy 2:26 44
Discern good and evil
  Hebrews 5:14 65
Discernment and understanding
  Proverbs 2:3 65
Earth's lower parts
  Psalm 63:9 72
Edification
  Ephesians 4:29 3
Entities (four)
  Ephesians 6:12 70

Eternal life
  John 10:28 1
Eternal Life
  Romans 6:23 39
Faith
  Hebrews 11:1 32
Faith and fasting
  Matthew 17:18-21 26
Faith—ask without doubt
  James 1:6-8 32
Faithful in little gets much
  Luke 19:17 66
Fall by the sword
  Psalm 63:9-10 73
Fear
  2 Timothy 1:7 45
Fear—love casts out
  1 John 4:18 45
Fight the good fight
  1 Timothy 6:12a 2
Fire-throw into
  John 15:6 38
Forget and reach forward
  Philippians 3:13 30
Forgive or not get forgiven
  Mark 11:26 19
Free indeed
  John 8:36 89
Fruit of the Spirit
  Galatians 5:22-23 86
Gap stander
  Ezekiel 22:30 53
Gift diversity
  1 Corinthians 12:4, 10, 11 65
God-Adonai Lord-Yehovah
  Exodus 18:1 6
God hears
  1 John 5:14-15 51
God is light
  1 John 1:5 33
God's peace
  Philippians 4:7 127
Good-doing
  Galatians 6:9 2

Good gift-perfect gift
  James 1:17 29
Healed by Jesus's stripes
  1 Peter 2:24 20
  Isaiah 53:5 20
Holy Spirit helper
  John 14:26 39
Jabez's prayer
  1 Chronicles 4:10 7
Jesus at the door
  Revelations 3:20 38
Jesus—believe and not perish
  John 3:14-15 125
Jesus is the light
  John 8:12 33
Justice for adversary
  Luke 18:1-8 34
Knowledge-lack-destroyed
  Hosea 4:5 68
Lack anything—ask
  James 1:5-6 25
Life more abundant
  John 10:10 45
Light cancels dark
  John 12:46 123
Light/lamp is the eye
  Luke 11:34-36 123
Light of life
  John 8:12 122
Light shines
  John 1:5 33
Living stone
  1 Peter 2:4-5 60
Lord-rock, fortress, deliverer
  Psalm 18:2 43
Lord-YHWH strong tower
  Proverbs 18:10 5
Meditate on these things
  Philippians 4:8 31
Mystery of God's will
  Ephesians 1:9 66
Net laid
  Psalm 31:4 44

ABOUT THE AUTHOR

Janis M. Betz became an ordained minister for Deliverance and Healing in 2006 at City of Light / Hunter Ministries. There she sat under the teaching of Frances and Charles Hunter. Janis operates in her discernment and intuitive gifting with her clients to gain spiritual knowledge to pray for them for deliverance and healing.

Janis started Spiritual Journey Fellowship, LLC in November 2021 as an extension of the healing services of Healthy Journey, Inc. She uses prayer to release cellular disturbances created by embedded negative emotions and memories, which leads to cellular dysfunction and disease. She saw a strong desire for her clients to go deeper into having a greater prayer impact for not only themselves but for others.

In September 1997, Janis founded Healthy Journey out of a burden to help people become well from illnesses related to diet and living habit choices. In January 2003, Healthy Journey became incorporated. Janis received her Nursing diploma from the Reading Hospital School of Nursing in 1984. She received her Bachelor of Science degree in Nursing in 1991 at Kutztown University. She has studied nutrition and lifestyle and its affects on health for many years. Janis has written three other books, The Journey to Ultimate Health; Your Healthy Journey Manual (Recipes & Protocols); and Deliverance & Healing Manual. She is also a workshop and seminar speaker.